PRAYER

PRAYER

JOHN BUNYAN

THE BANNER OF TRUTH TRUST

THE BANNER OF TRUTH TRUST
3 Murrayfield Road, Edinburgh EH12 6EL
PO Box 621, Carlisle, Pennsylvania 17013, USA

*

'Praying in the Spirit' first published 1662
'The Throne of Grace' first published 1692
First published in one volume by the
Banner of Truth Trust 1965
Reprinted 1989
Reprinted 1991
Reprinted 1995
Reprinted 1999
ISBN 0 85151 090 6

*

Printed and bound in Great Britain
by MPG Books Ltd, Bodmin, Cornwall

PUBLISHERS' FOREWORD

Two closely related works by John Bunyan on prayer are here brought together.

The first, originally published in 1662 under the title *I will pray with the spirit and with the understanding also*; or *A Discourse Touching Prayer*, was sent forth from Bedford gaol, where Bunyan later had 'the immortal dream'. Imprisoned for, among other things, his opposition to using the forms found in the Book of Common Prayer, it is not surprising to discover him writing on the true nature of prayer and contending that it must be the spontaneous utterance of the heart. Although shaped in some fashion by the historical context this is nevertheless a deeply spiritual work by a man to whom prayer was a real grappling of the soul with Almighty God.

The second work, *The Saints' Privilege and Profit*; or, *The Throne of Grace*, is based on the invitation in Hebrews 4. 16 to come boldly to the throne of grace. It was one of ten manuscripts which Bunyan had left prepared for the press at his death. Charles Doe published it in the first folio edition of Bunyan's Works in 1692.

These two works appear alongside one another in what is generally recognized as the best edition of Bunyan's Works, that collected and edited by George Offor. We have followed the Offor text for this reprint although where it was considered necessary we have modernized an expression and clarified an obscurity. Divisions and sub-headings have been amplified.

CONTENTS

I
PRAYING IN THE SPIRIT

'I will pray with the spirit, and I will pray with the understanding also.'

1 Cor. 14. 15

Prayer is an ordinance of God to be used both in public and private; yea, such an ordinance as brings those that have the spirit of supplication into great familiarity with God. It is also so prevalent an action that it gets from God, both for the person that prays, and for them that are prayed for, great things. It is the opener of the heart of God, and a means by which the soul, though empty, is filled. By prayer the Christian can open his heart to God, as to a friend, and obtain fresh testimony of God's friendship to him. I might spend many words in distinguishing between public and private prayer, as also between that in the heart, and that with the vocal voice. Something also might be said on the distinction between the gifts and graces of prayer; but I shall confine myself at this time to showing you the very heart of prayer, without which, all your lifting up, both of hands and eyes and voices, will be to no purpose at all. 'I will pray with the Spirit.'

The method that I shall follow at this time shall be:

First, To show you what true prayer is.

Secondly, To show you what it is to pray with the Spirit?

Thirdly, What it is to pray with the Spirit and understanding also.

Fourthly, To make some short use and application of what shall be spoken.

I

WHAT TRUE PRAYER IS

Prayer is a sincere, sensible, affectionate pouring out of the heart or soul to God, through Christ, in the strength and assistance of the Holy Spirit, for such things as God has promised, or according to his Word, for the good of the church, with submission in faith to the will of God.

In this description there are these seven things. Prayer is (1) a sincere; (2) a sensible; (3) an affectionate, pouring out of the soul to God, through Christ; (4) by the strength or assistance of the Spirit; (5) for such things as God has promised, or, according to his Word; (6) for the good of the church; (7) with submission in faith to the will of God.

1. For the first of these, it is a *sincere* pouring out of the soul to God.

Sincerity is such a grace as runs through all the graces of God in us, and through all the actings of a Christian, and has the sway in them too, or else their actings are not regarded of God. David speaks particularly of sincerity when he mentions prayer: 'I cried unto him with my mouth, and he was extolled with my tongue. If I regard iniquity in my heart, the Lord will not hear me (Ps. 66. 17, 18). Part of the exercise of prayer is sincerity, without which God does not accept it as prayer. (Ps. 16. 1–4). 'Ye shall seek me and find *me*, when ye shall search for me with all your heart' (Jer. 29. 12, 13). The want of this made the Lord reject the prayers of those mentioned in Hos. 7. 14, where he says, 'They have not cried unto

[13]

me with their heart,' that is, in sincerity, 'when they howled upon their beds.' It is rather for a pretence, for a show in hypocrisy, to be seen of men, and applauded for the same that they pray. Sincerity was that which Christ commended in Nathaniel, when he was under the fig tree. 'Behold, an Israelite indeed, in whom is no guile' (John 1. 47). Probably this good man was pouring out his soul to God in prayer under the fig tree, and that in a sincere and unfeigned spirit before the Lord. The prayer that has this in it as one of the principal ingredients is the prayer that God regards. Thus, 'The prayer of the upright is his delight' (Prov. 15. 8).

And why must sincerity be one of the essentials of prayer which is accepted of God? Because sincerity carries the soul in all simplicity to open its heart to God, and to tell him the case plainly, without equivocation; to condemn itself plainly, without dissembling; to cry to God heartily, without complimenting. 'I have surely heard Ephraim bemoaning himself thus; Thou hast chastised me, and I was chastised, as a bullock unaccustomed to the yoke. (Jer. 31. 18). Sincerity is the same in a corner alone, as it is before the face of all the world. It knows not how to wear two masks, one for an appearance before men, and another for private use. It must have God, and be with him in the duty of prayer. It is not a lip-labour that it regards, for sincerity, like God, looks at the heart, and that is where prayer comes from, if it be true prayer.

2. It is a sincere and *sensible* pouring out of the heart or soul.

It is not, as many take it to be, a few babbling, prating, complimentary expressions, but a sensible feeling in the heart. Prayer has in it a sensibleness of diverse things; sometimes sense of sin, sometimes of mercy received, sometimes of the readiness of God to give mercy.

(1) A sense of the want of mercy, by reason of the danger of sin. The soul, I say, feels, and from feeling sighs, groans, and breaks at the heart. For right prayer bubbles out of the heart when it is overcome with grief and bitterness, as blood is forced out of the flesh by reason of some heavy burden that lies upon it

[14]

(1 Sam. 1. 10. Ps. 69. 3). David roars, cries, weeps, faints at heart, fails at the eyes, loses his moisture (Ps. 38. 8–10). Hezekiah mourns like a dove (Is. 38. 14). Ephraim bemoans himself (Jer. 31. 18). Peter weeps bitterly (Matt. 26. 75). Christ has strong cryings and tears (Heb. 5. 7.) And all this from <u>a sense of the justice of God, the guilt of sin, the pains of hell and destruction.</u> 'The sorrows of death compassed me, and the pains of hell gat hold upon me: I found trouble and sorrow. Then called I upon the name of the Lord' (Ps. 116. 3, 4). And in another place, 'My sore ran in the night' (Ps. 77. 2). Again, 'I am bowed down greatly; I go mourning all the day long' (Ps. 38. 6). In all these instances, you may see that prayer carries in it a sensible feeling, and that first from <u>a sense of sin.</u>

(2) Sometimes there is a sweet sense of <u>mercy received</u>; encouraging, comforting, strengthening, enlivening, enlightening mercy. Thus David pours out his soul, to bless, and praise, and admire the great God for his loving-kindness to such poor vile wretches. 'Bless the Lord, O my soul; and all that is within me bless his holy name. Bless the Lord, O my soul, and forget not all his benefits. Who forgiveth all thine iniquities, who healeth all thy diseases; who redeemeth thy life from destruction; who crowneth thee with loving-kindness and tender mercies; who satisfieth thy mouth with good things, so that thy youth is renewed like the eagle's' (Ps. 103. 1–4). And thus is the prayer of saints sometimes turned into <u>praise and thanksgiving, and yet is still prayer.</u> This is a mystery; God's people pray with their praises, as it is written, 'Be careful for nothing, but in every thing by prayer, and supplication, with thanksgiving, let your requests be made known unto God' (Phil. 4. 6). A sensible thanksgiving for mercies received is a mighty prayer in the sight of God; it prevails with him unspeakably.

(3) In prayer there is sometimes in the soul a sense of <u>mercy to be received.</u> This again sets the soul aflame. 'Thou, O Lord of hosts,' says David, 'hast revealed to thy servant, saying I will build thee an house; therefore hath thy servant found in his heart to pray unto thee' (2 Sam. 7. 27). This provoked Jacob, David, Daniel, with others, <u>not by fits and starts, nor yet in a</u>

[15]

foolish frothy way, but mightily, fervently, and continually, to groan out their conditions before the Lord, as being sensible of their wants, their misery, and the willingness of God to show mercy (Gen. 32. 10, 11; Dan. 9. 3, 4).

3. Prayer is a sincere, sensible, and *an affectionate pouring out of the soul to God*.

(1) O, what heat, strength, life, vigour, and *affection* there is in true prayer! 'As the hart panteth after the water-brooks, so panteth my soul after thee, O God' (Ps. 42. 1). 'I have longed after thy precepts' (Ps. 119. 40). 'I have longed for thy salvation' (Ps. 17. 4). 'My soul longeth, yea, even fainteth, for the courts of the Lord; my heart and my flesh crieth out for the living God' (Ps. 84. 2). 'My soul breaketh for the longing *that it hath* unto thy judgments at all times' (Ps. 119. 20). O what affection is here discovered in prayer! You have the same in Daniel. 'O Lord, hear; O Lord, forgive; O Lord, hearken and do; defer not, for thine own sake, O my God' (Dan. 9. 19). Every syllable carries a mighty vehemency in it. This is called the fervent, or the working prayer, by James. And so again, 'And being in an agony, he prayed more earnestly' (Luke 22. 44). He had his affections more and more drawn out after God for his helping hand. O how wide are the most of men with their prayers from this prayer! Alas! the greatest part of men make no conscience at all of the duty; and as for them that do, it is to be feared that many of them are very great strangers to a sincere, sensible, and affectionate pouring out their hearts or souls to God. They content themselves with a little lip-labour and bodily exercise, mumbling over a few imaginary prayers. When the affections are indeed engaged in prayer, then the whole man is engaged, and that in such sort that the soul will spend itself, as it were, rather than go without that good desired, even communion and solace with Christ. And hence it is that the saints have spent their strength, and lost their lives, rather than go without the blessing (Ps. 69. 3; 38. 9, 10; Gen. 32. 24, 26).

All this is too evident by the ignorance, profaneness, and spirit of envy that reign in the hearts of those men that are so

[16]

hot for the forms, and not the power of praying. Few among them know what it is to be born again, to have communion with the Father through the Son; to feel the power of grace sanctifying their hearts. For all their prayers, they still live cursed, drunken, whorish, and abominable lives, full of malice, envy, deceit, persecuting the dear children of God. O what a dreadful judgment is coming upon them! a judgment from which all their hypocritical assembling themselves together, with all their prayers, shall never be able to help them against, or shelter them from.

Prayer is a *pouring out* of the heart or soul. There is in prayer an unbosoming of a man's self, an opening of the heart to God, an affectionate pouring out of the soul in requests, sighs, and groans. 'All my desire is before thee,' says David, 'and my groaning is not hid from thee' (Ps. 38. 9). And again, 'My soul thirsteth for God, for the living God. When shall I come and appear before God? When I remember these things, I pour out my soul in me' (Ps. 42. 2, 4). Mark, 'I pour out my soul.' It is an expression signifying that in prayer there goes the very life and whole strength to God. As in another place, 'Trust in him at all times; ye people, pour out your heart before him' (Ps. 62. 8). This is the prayer to which the promise is made, for the delivering of a poor creature out of captivity and thraldom. 'If from thence thou shalt seek the Lord thy God, thou shalt find him, if thou seek him with all thy heart and with all thy soul' Deut. 4. 29).

Again, prayer is a pouring out of the heart or soul *to God*. This shows also the excellency of the spirit of prayer. It is the great God to which it goes. 'When shall I come and appear before God?' And it argues that the soul that thus prays indeed, sees an emptiness in all things under heaven; that in God alone there is rest and satisfaction for the soul. 'Now she that is a widow, indeed, and desolate, trusteth in God' (1 Tim. 5. 5). So says David, 'In thee, O Lord, do I put my trust; let me never be put to confusion. Deliver me in thy righteousness, and cause me to escape; incline thine ear to me, and save me. Be thou my strong habitation, whereunto I may continually resort: for thou *art* my rock and my fortress; deliver me, O my God, out of the hand of the unrighteous and cruel man. For thou *art* my hope, O Lord God, *thou art* my trust from my youth' (Ps. 71. 1–5). Many speak of God; but right prayer makes God the hope, stay, and all. True prayer sees nothing substantial, and worth the looking after, but God. And that, as I said before, it does in a sincere, sensible, and affectionate way.

Again, prayer is a sincere, sensible, affectionate pouring out of the heart or soul to God, *through Christ*. This 'through Christ' must needs be added, or else it must be questioned, whether it is prayer, though in appearance it be never so eminent and eloquent.

Christ is the way through whom the soul has admittance to God, and without whom it is impossible that so much as one desire should come into the ears of the Lord of Sabaoth (John 14. 6). 'If ye shall ask anything in my name;' 'whatsoever ye shall ask the Father in my name, I will do it.' This was Daniel's way in praying for the people of God; he did it in the name of Christ. 'Now therefore, O our God, hear the prayer of thy servant, and his supplications, and cause thy face to shine upon thy sanctuary that is desolate, for the Lord's sake' (Dan. 9. 17). And so David, 'For thy name's sake—that is, for thy Christ's sake—'pardon mine iniquity, for it is great' (Ps. 25. 11). But now it is not every one that makes mention of Christ's name in prayer that does indeed, and in truth, effectually pray to God in the name of Christ, or through him. This coming to God through Christ is the hardest part of prayer. A man may be sensible of his condition, and sincerely desire mercy, and yet not be able to come to God by Christ. The man that comes to God by Christ must first have the knowledge of him; 'for he that cometh to God, must believe that he is' (Heb. 11. 6). And so he that comes to God through Christ, must be enabled to know Christ. Lord, says Moses, 'show me now thy way, that I may know thee' (Ex. 32. 13).

This Christ, none but the Father can reveal (Matt. 11. 27). And to come through Christ is for the sinner to be enabled of God to hide himself under the shadow of the Lord Jesus, as a man hides himself under a thing for safeguard (Matt. 16. 16). Hence it is that David so often terms Christ his shield, buckler, tower, fortress, rock of defence (Ps. 18. 2; 27. 1; 28. 1). Not only because by him he overcame his enemies, but because through him he found favour with God the Father. And so God says to Abraham, 'Fear not, I am thy shield' (Gen. 15. 1). The man then that comes to God through Christ must have faith, by which he puts on Christ, and in him appears before God. Now he that has faith is born of God, and so becomes one of the sons of God; by virtue of which he is joined to Christ, and made a member of Christ (John 3. 5, 7; 1. 12). And, therefore, he, as a member of Christ, comes to God; I say, as a member of Christ, so that God looks on that man as part of Christ, part of his body, flesh, and bones, united to him by election, conversion, enlightenment, the Spirit being conveyed into the heart of that man by God (Eph. 5. 30). So that now he comes to God in Christ's merits, in his blood, righteousness, victory, intercession, and so stands before him, being 'accepted in the Beloved' (Eph. 1. 6). And because this poor creature is thus a member of the Lord Jesus, and under this consideration has admittance to God; therefore, by virtue of this union also is the Holy Spirit conveyed into him, whereby he is able to pour out his soul before God.

4. Prayer is a sincere, sensible, affectionate, pouring out of the heart or soul to God through Christ, *by the strength or assistance of the Spirit.*

These things so depend one upon another that it is impossible that it should be prayer without a joint concurrence of them; for though it be never so eloquent, yet without these things, it is only such prayer as is rejected of God. For without a sincere, sensible, affectionate, pouring out of the heart to God, it is but lip-labour; and if it be not through Christ, it falls far short of ever sounding well in the ears of God. So also, if it be not in the strength and by the assistance of the Spirit, it is but like the sons of Aaron, offering strange fire (Lev. 10. 1, 2). But more of this later. In the meantime I say that which is not petitioned through the teaching and assistance of the Spirit cannot be 'according to *the will of* God' (Rom. 8. 26, 27).

5. Prayer is a sincere, sensible, affectionate pouring out of the heart, or soul, to God, through Christ, in the strength and assistance of the Spirit, *for such things as God has promised* (Matt. 6. 6–8).

Prayer is only true when it is within the compass of God's Word; it is blasphemy, or at best vain babbling, when the petition is unrelated to the Book. David therefore in his prayer kept his eye on the Word of God. 'My soul,' says he, 'cleaveth to the dust; quicken me according to thy word.' And again, 'My soul melteth for heaviness, strengthen thou me according unto thy word' (Ps. 119. 25–28. See also verses 41, 42, 58, 65, 74, 81, 82, 107, 147, 154, 169, 170). And, 'remember the word unto thy servant, upon which thou hast caused me to hope' (ver. 49). And indeed the Holy Ghost does not immediately quicken and stir up the heart of the Christian without, but by, with, and through the Word, by bringing that to the heart, and by opening that, whereby the man is provoked to go to the Lord, and to tell him how it is with him; and also to argue, and supplicate, according to the Word. Thus it was with Daniel that mighty prophet of the Lord. He, understanding by books that the captivity of the children of Israel was nearing its end, then, according unto that word, he makes his prayer to God. 'I Daniel,' says he, 'understood by books,' viz., the writings of Jeremiah, 'the number of the years whereof the word of the Lord came to Jeremiah, that he would accomplish seventy years in the desolations of Jerusalem. And I set my face to the Lord God, to seek by prayer and supplications, with fasting, and sackcloth, and ashes' (Ch. 9. 2, 3).

As the Spirit is the helper and the governor of the soul, when it prays according to the will of God; so it guides by and according to the Word of God and his promise. Hence it is that our Lord Jesus Christ himself did make a stop, although his life lay at stake for it. 'I could now pray to my Father, and he should give me more than twelve legions of angels; but how then must the Scripture be fulfilled that thus it must be?' (Matt. 26. 53, 54). Were there but a word for it in the Scripture, I should soon be out of the hands of mine enemies, I should be helped by angels; but the Scripture will not warrant this kind of praying, for that says otherwise.

It is a praying then according to the Word and promise. The Spirit by the Word must direct, in the manner, as well as in the matter of prayer. 'I will pray with the Spirit, and I will pray with the understanding also' (1 Cor. 14. 15). But there is no understanding without the Word. For if they reject the word of the Lord, 'what wisdom is in them?' (Jer. 8. 9.)

6. For the good of the Church.

This clause covers whatsoever tends either to the honour of God, Christ's advancement, or his people's benefit. For God, and Christ, and his people are so linked together that if the good of the one be prayed for, the others must needs be included. As Christ is in the Father, so the saints are in Christ; and he that touches the saints, touches the apple of God's eye. Therefore pray for the peace of Jerusalem, and you pray for all that is required of you. For Jerusalem will never be in perfect peace until she be in heaven; and there is nothing that Christ more desires than to have her there. That also is the place that God through Christ has given her. He then that prays for the peace and good of Zion, or the church, asks that in prayer which Christ has purchased with his blood; and also that which the Father has given to him as the price thereof. Now he that prays for this, must pray for abundance of grace for the church, for help against all its temptations; that God would let nothing be too hard for it; that all things might work together for its good; that God would keep his children blameless and harmless, the sons of God, to his glory, in the midst of a crooked and perverse nation. And this is the substance of Christ's own prayer in John 17. And all Paul's prayers run that way, as one of his prayers eminently shows: 'And this I pray, that your love may abound yet more and more in knowledge, and in all judgment;

that ye may approve things that are excellent; that ye may be sincere, and without offence, till the day of Christ. Being filled with the fruits of righteousness, which are by Jesus Christ unto the glory and praise of God' (Phil. 1. 9–11). But a short prayer, you see, and yet full of good desires for the church, from the beginning to the end; that it may stand and go on, and that in the most excellent frame of spirit, even without blame, sincere, and without offence, until the day of Christ, let its temptations or persecutions be what they will (Eph. 1. 16–21; 3. 14–19; Col. 1. 9–13).

7. And because, as I said, prayer *submits to the will of God*, and says, Thy will be done, as Christ has taught (Matt. 6. 10); therefore the people of the Lord in all humility are to lay themselves and their prayers, and all that they have, at the foot of their God, to be disposed of by him as he in his heavenly wisdom sees best. Yet not doubting but God will answer the desire of his people that way that shall be most for their advantage and his glory. When the saints therefore pray with submission to the will of God, it does not argue that they are to doubt or question God's love and kindness to them. But because they at all times are not so wise, but that sometimes Satan may get advantage of them, as to tempt them to pray for that which, if they had it, would neither prove to God's glory nor his people's good. 'Yet this is the confidence that we have in him, that if we ask anything according to his will, he heareth us; and if we know that he hear us, whatsoever we ask, we know that we have the petitions that we desired of him,' that is, we asking in the Spirit of grace and supplication (1 John 5. 14, 15). For, as I said before, that petition that is not put up in and through the Spirit, is not to be answered, because it is beside the will of God. For the Spirit only knows that, and so consequently knows how to pray according to that will of God. 'For what man knoweth the things of a man, save the spirit of man which is in him? even so the things of God knoweth no man but the Spirit of God' (1 Cor. 2. 11). But more of this hereafter.

2

WHAT IT IS TO PRAY WITH THE SPIRIT

'I will pray with the Spirit.' Now to pray with the Spirit—
for that denotes the praying man, and none else, so as to be
accepted of God—it is for a man, as aforesaid, sincerely and
sensibly, with affection, to come to God through Christ, which
sincere, sensible, and affectionate coming must be by the working of God's Spirit.

There is no man nor church in the world that can come to
God in prayer, but by the assistance of the Holy Spirit. 'For
through Christ we all have access by one Spirit unto the Father'
(Eph. 2. 18). Wherefore Paul says, 'For we know not what we
should pray for as we ought; but the Spirit itself maketh intercession for us with groanings which cannot be uttered. And he
that searcheth the hearts knoweth what is the mind of the
Spirit, because he maketh intercession for the saints according
to the will of God' (Rom. 8. 26, 27). And because there is in this
Scripture so full a discovery of the spirit of prayer, and of man's
inability to pray without it; therefore I shall in a few words
comment upon it.

'For we.' Consider first the person speaking, even Paul, and,
in his person, all the apostles. We apostles, we extraordinary
officers, the wise master-builders, some of whom have been
caught up into paradise (Rom. 15. 16; 1 Cor. 3. 10; 2 Cor. 12. 4).
'We know not what we should pray for.' Surely there is no man
but will confess that Paul and his companions were as able to
have done any work for God, as any pope or proud prelate in

the church of Rome, and could as well have made a Common Prayer Book as those who at first composed this; as being not a whit behind them either in grace or gifts.

'For we know not what we should pray for.' We know not the matter of the things for which we should pray, neither the object to whom we pray, nor the medium by or through whom we pray; none of these things know we, but by the help and assistance of the Spirit. Should we pray for communion with God through Christ? Should we pray for faith, for justification by grace, and a truly sanctified heart? None of these things know we. 'For what man knoweth the things of a man, save the spirit of man which is in him? even so the things of God knoweth no man, but the Spirit of God' (1 Cor. 2. 11). But here, alas! the apostles speak of inward and spiritual things, which the world knows not (Is. 29. 11).

Again, as they know not the matter of prayer, without the help of the Spirit; so neither know they the manner thereof without the same; and therefore he adds, 'We know not what we should pray for as we ought;' but the Spirit helps our infirmities, with sighs and groans which cannot be uttered. Mark here, they could not so well and so fully succeed in the manner of performing this duty, as these in our days think they can.

The apostles, when they were at the best, yea when the Holy Ghost assisted them, yet then they were fain to come off with sighs and groans, falling short of expressing their mind, but with sighs and groans which cannot be uttered.

'For we know not what we should pray for as we ought.' Mark this, 'as we ought.' For the not thinking of this word, or at least the not understanding it in the spirit and truth of it, has occasioned some men to devise, as Jeroboam did, another way of worship, both for matter and manner, than is revealed in the Word of God (1 Kgs. 12. 26–33). But, says Paul, we must pray as we ought; and this we cannot do by all the art, skill, cunning, and device of men or angels. 'For we know not what we should pray for as we ought, but the Spirit;' nay, further, it must be 'the Spirit itself' that helps our infirmities; not the Spirit and man's lusts. What man of his own brain may imagine

[24]

and devise, is one thing, and what they are commanded, and ought to do, is another.

Many ask and have not, because they ask amiss; and so are never the nearer the enjoying of those things they petition for (Jas. 4. 3). It is not to pray at random that will cause God to answer. While prayer is making, God is searching the heart to see from what root and spirit it arises (1 John 5. 14). 'And he that searcheth the heart knoweth,' that is, approves only, the meaning 'of the Spirit, because he maketh intercession for the saints according to the will of God.' For in that which is according to his will only, he hears us, and in nothing else. And it is the Spirit only that can teach us so to ask; it only being able to search out all things, even the deep things of God. Without which Spirit, though we had a thousand Common Prayer Books, yet we know not what we should pray for as we ought, being accompanied with those infirmities that make us absolutely incapable of such a work. Which infirmities, although it is a hard thing to name them all, yet some of them are these that follow.

1. Without the Spirit man is so infirm that he cannot, with all other means whatsoever, be enabled to think one right saving thought of God, of Christ, or of his blessed things; and therefore he says of the wicked, 'God is not in all his thoughts,' (Ps. 10. 4); unless it be that they imagine him altogether such a one as themselves (Ps. 50. 20). For 'every imagination of the thoughts of his heart was only evil,' and that 'continually' Gen. 6. 5; 8. 21. They then not being able to conceive aright of God to whom they pray, of Christ through whom they pray, nor of the things for which they pray, as is before showed, how shall they be able to address themselves to God, without the Spirit helping this infirmity?

The Spirit Himself is the revealer of these things to poor souls, and that which doth give us to understand them; wherefore Christ tells his disciples, when he promised to send the Spirit, the Comforter, 'He shall take of mine and show unto you;' as if he had said, I know you are naturally dark and

[25]

ignorant as to the understanding of any of my things; though you try this course and the other, yet your ignorance will still remain, the vail is spread over your heart, and there is none can take away the same, nor give you spiritual understanding, but the Spirit. Right prayer must, in the outward expression, as in the inward intention, come from what the soul apprehends in the light of the Spirit; otherwise it is condemned as vain and an abomination, because the heart and tongue do not go along jointly in the same, neither indeed can they, unless the Spirit help our infirmities (Mark 7; Prov. 28. 9; Is. 29. 13). And this David knew full well, which made him cry, 'Lord, open thou my lips, and my mouth shall show forth thy praise' (Ps. 51. 15). I suppose that David could speak and express himself as well as others, nay, as any in our generation, as is clearly manifested by his word and his works. Nevertheless when this good man, this prophet, comes into God's worship, then the Lord must help, or he can do nothing. 'Lord, open thou my lips, and' then 'my mouth shall show forth thy praise.' He could not speak one right word, except the Spirit himself gave utterance. 'For we know not what we should pray for as we ought, but the Spirit itself helpeth our infirmities.'

2. It must be a praying with the Spirit, that is, effectual praying; because without that, as men are senseless, so are they hypocritical, cold, and unseemly in their prayers; and so they, with their prayers, are both rendered abominable to God (Matt. 23. 14; Mark 12. 40; Luke 18. 11, 12. Is. 58. 2, 3). It is not the excellency of the voice, nor the seeming affection and earnestness of him that prays, that is anything regarded of God without it. For man, as man, is so full of all manner of wickedness that as he cannot keep a word, or thought, so much less a piece of prayer clean and acceptable to God through Christ; and for this cause the Pharisees, with their prayers, were rejected. No doubt they were excellently able to express themselves in words, and that at great length; but they had not the Spirit of Jesus Christ to help them, and therefore they did what they did with their infirmities or weaknesses only, and so fell short of a

[26]

sincere, sensible, affectionate pouring out of their souls to God, through the strength of the Spirit. The prayer that goes to heaven is the one that is sent thither in the strength of the Spirit.

3. Nothing but the Spirit can show a man clearly his misery by nature, and so put a man into a posture of prayer. Talk is *Conviction* but talk, as we are accustomed to say, and so it is but mouth-worship, if there be not a sense of misery, and that effectually too. O the cursed hypocrisy that is in most hearts, and that accompanies many thousands of praying men that would be so looked upon in this day, and all for want of a sense of their misery! But when the Spirit works he sweetly shows the soul its misery, where it is, and what is like to become of it, also the intolerableness of that condition. For it is the Spirit that effectually convinces of sin and misery, without the Lord Jesus, and so puts the soul into a sweet, serious, sensible, affectionate way of praying to God according to his Word (John 16. 7–9).

4. If men did see their sins, yet without the help of the Spirit they would not pray. For they would run away from God, with *Mercy.* Cain and Judas, and utterly despair of mercy, were it not for the Spirit. When a man is indeed sensible of his sin, and God's curse, then it is a hard thing to persuade him to pray; for, says his heart, 'There is no hope,' it is in vain to seek God (Jer. 2. 25; 18. 12). I am so vile, so wretched, and so cursed a creature that I shall never be regarded! Now here comes the Spirit, and stays the soul, helps it to hold up its face to God, by letting into the heart some small sense of mercy to encourage it to go to God, and hence he is called 'the Comforter' (John 14. 26).

5. It must be in or with the Spirit; for without that no man *the Way* can know how he should come to God the right way. Men may *to God* easily say that they come to God in his Son, but it is the hardest thing of a thousand to come to God aright and in his own way, without the Spirit. It is 'the Spirit' that 'searcheth all things, yea, the deep things of God' (1 Cor. 2. 10). It is the Spirit that

must show us the way of coming to God, and also what there is in God that makes him desirable. 'I pray thee,' says Moses, 'show me now thy way, that I may know thee' (Exod. 33. 13). And, He shall take of mine, and 'show it unto you' (John 16. 14).

6. Because without the Spirit, though a man did see his misery, and also the way to come to God; yet he would never be able to claim a share in either God, Christ, or mercy, with God's approbation. O how great a task it is, for a poor soul that becomes sensible of sin and the wrath of God, to say in faith but this one word, 'Father!' I tell you, however hypocrites think, yet the Christian that is so indeed finds all the difficulty in this very thing; he cannot say God is his Father. O! says he, I dare not call him Father; and hence it is that the Spirit must be sent into the hearts of God's people for this very thing, to cry Abba, Father: it being too great a work for any man to do knowingly and believingly without it (Gal. 4. 6). When I say knowingly, I mean, knowing what it is to be a child of God, and to be born again. And when I say believingly, I mean, for the soul to believe, and that from good experience, that the work of grace is wrought in him. This is the right calling of God Father; and not as many do, to say in a babbling way, the Lord's prayer (so called) by heart, as it lies in the words of the book. No, here is the life of prayer, when in or with the Spirit, a man being made sensible of sin, and how to come to the Lord for mercy, he comes, I say, in the strength of the Spirit, and cries Father. That one word spoken in faith is better than a thousand prayers, as men call them, written and read in a formal, cold, luke-warm way.

O how far short are the people of being sensible of this, who count it enough to teach themselves and children to say the Lord's prayer, the creed, with other sayings; when, as God knows, they are senseless of themselves, their misery, or what it is to be brought to God through Christ! Ah, poor soul! study your misery, and cry to God to show you your confused blindness and ignorance, before you be too ready in calling God your Father, or teaching your children either so to say. And know,

[28]

that to say God is your Father, in a way of prayer or confer-
ence, without any experiment of the work of grace on your
souls, it is to say you are Jews and are not, and so do lie. You
say, Our Father; God says, You blaspheme! You say you are
Jews, that is, true Christians; God says You lie! 'Behold I will
make them of the synagogue of Satan, which say they are
Jews, and are not, but do lie' (Rev. 3. 9). 'And I know the blasphemy of them that say they are Jews, and are not, but are the
synagogue of Satan' (Rev. 2. 9). And so much the greater the
sin is, when the sinner boasts it with a pretended sanctity, as
the Jews did to Christ, in John chapter 8, which made Christ,
even in plain terms, to tell them their doom, for all their hypocritical pretences (vv. 41–45). And yet forsooth every cursed
whoremaster, thief, and drunkard, swearer, and perjured person—they that have not only been such in times past, but are
even so still—these I say, by some must be counted the only
honest men, and all because with their blasphemous throats,
and hypocritical hearts, they will come to church, and say,
'Our Father!' Nay further, these men, though every time they
say to God, Our Father, do most abominably blaspheme, yet
they must be compelled thus to pray. And because others that
are of more sober principles, scruple the truth of such vain
traditions, they are regarded as the only enemies of God and
the nation: whereas it is their own cursed superstition that
doth set the great God against them and cause him to count
them for his enemies (Is. 63. 10). And yet they commend, I say,
these wretches, although never so vile, if they close in with
their traditions, to be good churchmen and honest subjects;
while God's people are, as it has always been, regarded as a
turbulent, seditious, and factious people (Ezra 4. 12–16).

Therefore give me leave a little to reason with you, poor
blind, ignorant, foolish one.

(1) It may be your chief prayer is, 'Our Father which art in
heaven, &c.' Do you know the meaning of the very first words
of this prayer? Can you indeed, with the rest of the saints, cry,
Our Father? Are you truly born again? have you received the
spirit of adoption? Do you see yourself in Christ, and can you

[29]

come to God as a member of Christ? Or are you ignorant of these things, and yet dare you say, Our Father? Is not the devil your father? (John 8. 44). And do you not do the deeds of the flesh? and yet dare you say to God, Our Father? Nay, are you not a desperate persecutor of the children of God? have you not cursed them in your heart many a time? and yet do you out of your blasphemous throat suffer these words to come, even Our Father? He is their Father whom you hate and persecute. But as the devil presented himself amongst the sons of God (Job. 1. 6–7), when they were to present themselves before the Father, even our Father, so it is now. Because the saints are commanded to say, Our Father, therefore all the blind ignorant rabble in the world must also use the same words, Our Father.

(2) And do you indeed say, 'Hallowed be thy name' with your heart? Do you study, by all honest and lawful ways, to advance the name, holiness, and majesty of God? Do your heart and conversation agree with this passage? Do you strive to imitate Christ in all the works of righteousness, which God commands you, and prompts you to? It is so, if you are one that can truly with God's permission cry, 'Our Father'. Or is it not the least of your thoughts all the day? and do you not clearly make it appear that you are a cursed hypocrite, by condemning that with your daily practice, which you pretend in your praying with a dissembling tongue?

(3) Would you have the kingdom of God come indeed, and also his will to be done in earth as it is in heaven? nay, even though, according to the form, you say, Thy kingdom come, yet would it not make you ready to run mad, to hear the trumpet sound, to see the dead arise, and yourself just now to go and appear before God, to give an account of all the deeds you have done in the body? Nay, are not the very thoughts of it altogether displeasing to you? and if God's will should be done on earth as it is in heaven, must it not be your ruin? There is never a rebel in heaven against God, and if he should so deal on earth, must it not whirl you down to hell? Likewise with the rest of the petitions. Ah! how sadly would even those men look, and with what terror would they walk up and down

the world, if they did but know the lying and blaspheming that proceed out of their mouth, even in their most pretended sanctity? The Lord awaken you, and teach you, poor souls, in all humility, to take heed that you be not rash and unadvised with your heart, and much more with your mouth! When you appear before God, as the wise man says, 'Be not rash with thy mouth, and let not thine heart be hasty to utter anything (Eccles. 5. 2);' especially to call God Father, without some blessed experience when you come before God.

7. It must be a praying with the Spirit if it be accepted, because there is nothing but the Spirit that can lift up the soul or heart to God in prayer: 'The preparations of the heart in man, and the answer of the tongue, is from the Lord' (Prov. 16. 1). That is, in every work for God, and especially in prayer, if the heart run with the tongue, it must be prepared by the Spirit of God. Indeed the tongue is very apt, of itself, to run without either fear or wisdom: but when it is the answer of the heart, and that such a heart as is prepared by the Spirit of God, then it speaks as God commands and desires.

They are mighty words of David, where he says, that he lifts his heart and his soul to God (Ps. 25. 1). It is a great work for any man without the strength of the Spirit, and therefore I conceive that this is one of the great reasons why the Spirit of God is called a Spirit of supplications (Zech. 12. 10), because he helps the heart when it supplicates indeed to do it; and therefore says Paul, 'Praying with all prayer and supplication in the Spirit' (Eph. 6. 18). And so in my text, 'I will pray with the Spirit.' Prayer, unless the heart be in it, is like a sound without life; and a heart, unless it be lifted up of the Spirit, will never pray to God.

8. As the heart must be lifted up by the Spirit, if it pray aright, so also it must be held up by the Spirit when it is up, if it is to continue to pray aright. I do not know what or how it is with others' hearts, whether they be lifted up by the Spirit of God, and so continued, or no: but this I am sure of, first, that it

[31]

is impossible that all the prayer books that men have made in the world, should lift up, or prepare the heart, for that is the work of the great God himself. And, in the second place, I am sure that they are as far from keeping it up, when it is up. And indeed here is the life of prayer, to have the heart kept with God in the duty. It was a great matter for Moses to keep his hands lifted up to God in prayer; but how much more then to keep the heart in it! (Exod. 17. 12.)

The want of this is that which God complains of; that men draw nigh to him with their mouth, and know him with their lips, but their hearts are far from him (Is. 29. 13; Ezek. 33. 31), but chiefly they that walk after the commandments and traditions of men, as the scope of Matthew 15. 8, 9 testifies. And verily, may I but speak my own experience, and from that tell you the difficulty of praying to God as I ought, it is enough to make your poor, blind, carnal men to entertain strange thoughts of me. For, as for my heart, when I go to pray, I find it so loth to go to God, and when it is with him, so loth to stay with him, that many times I am forced in my prayers, first to beg of God that he would take mine heart, and set it on himself in Christ, and when it is there, that he would keep it there. Nay, many times I know not what to pray for, I am so blind, nor how to pray, I am so ignorant; only, blessed be grace, the Spirit helps our infirmities (Ps. 86. 11).

O the starting-holes that the heart has in the time of prayer! None knows how many by-ways the heart has, and back-lanes, to slip away from the presence of God. How much pride also, if enabled with expressions! How much hypocrisy, if before others! And how little conscience is there made of prayer between God and the soul in secret, unless the Spirit of supplication be there to help! When the Spirit gets into the heart, then there is prayer indeed, and not till then.

9. The soul that rightly prays, it must be in and with the help and strength of the Spirit; because it is impossible that a man should express himself in prayer without it. By this I mean that

it is impossible that the heart, in a sincere and affectionate way, should pour out itself before God, with those groans and sighs that come from a truly praying heart, without the assistance of the Spirit. It is not the mouth that is the main thing to be looked at in prayer, but whether the heart is so full of affection and earnestness in prayer with God that it is impossible to express their sense and desire; for then a man desires indeed, when his desires are so strong, many, and mighty, that all the words, tears and groans that come from the heart cannot utter them: 'The Spirit helpeth our infirmities, and maketh intercession for us with' sighs and 'groanings which cannot be uttered' (Rom. 8. 26).

That is but poor prayer which is only one of words. A man that truly prays one prayer cannot express with his mouth or pen the unutterable desires, sense, affection, and longing that went to God in his prayer. The best prayers have often more groans than words: and those words that they have are but a lean and shallow representation of the heart, life, and spirit of prayer. You do not find any words of prayer that we read of, come out of the mouth of Moses, when he was gone out of Egypt, and was followed by Pharaoh, and yet he made heaven ring again with his cry (Exod. 14. 15). But it was inexpressible and unsearchable groans and cryings of his soul in and with the Spirit. God is the God of spirits, and his eyes look further than at the outside of our duties ((Num. 16. 22). Yet this is but little thought on by the most of them that would be looked upon as a praying people (1 Sam. 16. 7).

The nearer a man comes in any work that God commands him, to the doing of it according to God's will, so much the more hard and difficult it is; and the reason is, because man, as man, is not able to do it. But prayer, as aforesaid, is not only a duty, but one of the most eminent duties, and therefore so much the more difficult: therefore Paul knew what he said, when he wrote, 'I will pray with the Spirit.' He knew well it was not what others writ or said that could make him a praying person; nothing less than the Spirit could do it.

10. It must be with the Spirit, or else, as there will be a failing in the act itself, so there will be a failing, yea, a fainting, in the prosecution of the work. Prayer is an ordinance of God, that must continue with a soul so long as it is on this side glory. But, as I said before, it is not possible for a man to get up his heart to God in prayer; likewise it is as difficult to keep it there, without the assistance of the Spirit. And if so, then for a man to continue from time to time in prayer with God, it must of necessity be with the Spirit.

Christ tells us that men ought always to pray, and not to faint (Luke 18. 1). And again he tells us, that this is one definition of a hypocrite, that either he will not continue in prayer, or else if he do it, it will not be in the power, that is, in the spirit of prayer, but in the form, for a pretence only (Job 27. 10; Matt. 23. 14). It is the easiest thing of a hundred to fall from the power to the form, but it is the hardest thing of many to keep in the life, spirit, and power of any one duty, especially prayer; that is such a work, that a man without the help of the Spirit cannot so much as pray once, much less continue, without it, in a sweet praying frame, and in praying, so to pray as to have his prayers ascend into the ears of the Lord of sabaoth.

Jacob did not only begin, but held to it : 'I will not let thee go, unless thou bless me' (Gen. 32. 26). So did the rest of the godly (Hos. 12. 4). But this could not be without the spirit of prayer. It is through the Spirit that we have access to the Father (Eph. 2. 18).

There is a remarkable place in Jude, when he stirs up the saints by the judgment of God upon the wicked, to stand fast and continue to hold out in the faith of the gospel, as one excellent means thereto, without which he knew they would never be able to do it. Says he, 'Building up yourselves on your most holy faith, praying in the Holy Ghost' (Jude 20). As if he had said, Brethren, as eternal life is laid up for the persons that hold out, and for none other, so you cannot hold out unless you continue praying in the Spirit. The great cheat by means of which the devil and antichrist delude the world, is to make them continue in the form of any duty, the form of preaching, of hearing, or of praying. These are they that have 'a form of godliness, but deny the power thereof; from such turn away' (2 Tim. 3. 5).

3

WHAT IT IS TO PRAY WITH THE SPIRIT, AND WITH THE UNDERSTANDING

The apostle puts a clear distinction between praying with the Spirit and with the understanding; therefore when he says, 'he will pray with the Spirit,' he adds, 'and will pray with the understanding *also*.' This distinction was occasioned through the Corinthians not observing that it was their duty to do what they did to the edification of themselves and others too: whereas they did it for their own commendation. So I judge: for many of them having extraordinary gifts, for example, the speaking with divers tongues, therefore they were more for those mighty gifts than they were for the edifying of their brethren; which was the cause that Paul wrote this chapter to them, to let them understand, that though extraordinary gifts were excellent, yet to do what they did for the edification of the church was more excellent. For 'if I pray in an unknown tongue, my spirit prayeth, but my understanding,' and also the understanding of others, 'is unfruitful' (1 Cor. 14. 3, 4, 12, 19, 24, 25). Therefore, 'I will pray with the Spirit, and I will pray with the understanding also.'

It is expedient then that the understanding should be occupied in prayer, as well as the heart and mouth : 'I will pray with the Spirit, and I will pray with the understanding also.' That which is done with understanding, is done more effectually, sensibly, and heartily, as I shall show farther anon, than that which is done without it; which made the apostle pray for the Colossians, that God would fill them 'with the knowledge of his will, in all wisdom and spiritual understanding' (Col. 1. 9). And for the Ephesians, that God would give unto them 'the spirit of wisdom and revelation, in the knowledge of him' (Eph. 1. 17). And so for the Philippians, that God would make them abound 'in knowledge, and in all judgment' (Phil. 1. 9). A suitable understanding is good in everything a man undertakes, either civil or spiritual; and therefore it must be desired by all them that would be a praying people. I shall next show you what it is to pray with understanding.

Understanding is to be taken both for speaking in our mother-tongue, and also experimentally. I pass by the first, and treat only on the second.

For the making of right prayers, it is required that there should be a good or spiritual understanding in all them who pray to God.

1. To pray with understanding, is to pray as being instructed by the Spirit in the understanding of the want of those things which the soul is to pray for. Though a man be in never so much need of pardon of sin, and deliverance from wrath to come, yet if he understand not this, he will either not desire them at all, or else be so cold and lukewarm in his desires after them, that God will even loathe his frame of spirit in asking for them. Thus it was with the church of the Laodiceans. They lacked spiritual understanding; they knew not that they were poor, wretched, blind, and naked. The cause whereof made them, and all their services, so loathsome to Christ, that he threatens to spue them out of his mouth (Rev. 3. 16, 17). Men without understanding may say the same words in prayer as others do; but if there be an understanding in the one, and none in the other, there is, O there is a mighty difference in speaking the very same words! The one speaks from a spiritual understanding of those things that he in words desires, and the other words it only, and that is all.

[37]

2. Spiritual understanding espies in the heart of God a readiness and willingness to give those things to the soul that it stands in need of. David by this could guess at the very thoughts of God towards him (Ps. 40. 5). And thus it was with the woman of Canaan; by faith and a right understanding she discerned, beyond all the rough carriage of Christ, tenderness and willingness in his heart to save, which caused her to be vehement and earnest, yea, restless, until she enjoyed the mercy she stood in need of (Matt. 15. 22–28).

There is nothing that will press the soul more to seek after God, and to cry for pardon, than an understanding of the willingness that is in the heart of God to save sinners. If a man should see a pearl worth an hundred pounds lie in a ditch, yet if he understood not the value of it, he would lightly pass it by: but if he once get the knowledge of it, he would venture up to the neck for it. So it is with souls concerning the things of God: if a man once get an understanding of the worth of them, then his heart, nay, the very strength of his soul, runs after them, and he will never leave crying till he have them. The two blind men in the gospel, because they did certainly know that Jesus, who was going by them, was both able and willing to heal such infirmities as they were afflicted with: therefore they cried, and the more they were rebuked the more they cried (Matt 20. 29–31).

3. The understanding being spiritually enlightened, hereby is the way discovered through which the soul should come unto God; which gives great encouragement unto it. It is else with a poor soul, as with one who has a work to do, and if it be not done, the danger is great; if it be done, so is the advantage. But he knows not how to begin, nor how to proceed; and so, through discouragement, lets all alone, and runs the hazard.

4. The enlightened understanding sees largeness enough in the promises to encourage it to pray; which still adds to it strength to strength. As when men promise such and such things to all that will come for them, it is great encouragement

Promise

[38]

to those that know what promises are made, to come and ask for them.

5. The understanding being enlightened, way is made for the soul to come to God with suitable arguments, sometimes in a way of expostulation, as Jacob (Gen. 32. 9). Sometimes in a way of supplication, yet not in a verbal way only, but even from the heart there is forced by the Spirit, through the understanding, such effectual arguments as move the heart of God. When Ephraim gets a right understanding of his own unseemly behaviour towards the Lord, then he begins to bemoan himself (Jer. 31. 18–20). And in bemoaning himself, he uses such arguments with the Lord that it affects his heart, draws out forgiveness, and makes Ephraim pleasant in his eyes through Jesus Christ our Lord : 'I have surely heard Ephraim bemoaning himself thus,' saith God, 'Thou hast chastised me, and I was chastised; as a bullock unaccustomed to the yoke; turn thou me, and I shall be turned: for thou art the Lord my God. Surely after that I was turned, I repented, and after that I was instructed' (or had a right understanding of myself), 'I smote upon my thigh, I was ashamed; yea, even confounded; because I did bear the reproach of my youth.' These be Ephraim's complaints and bemoanings of himself; at which the Lord breaks forth into these heart-melting expressions, saying, 'Is Ephraim my dear son? Is he a pleasant child? For since I spake against him, I do earnestly remember him still; therefore my bowels are troubled for him; I will surely have mercy upon him, saith the Lord.' Thus, you see, that as it is required to pray with the Spirit, so it is to pray with the understanding also.

To illustrate what has been spoken by a similitude : suppose there should come two men begging to your door; the one is a poor, lame, wounded, and almost starved creature, the other is a healthy strong person; these two use the same words in their begging; the one says he is almost starved, so does the other: but the man that is indeed the poor, lame, or maimed person, he speaks with more sense, feeling, and understanding of the misery that is mentioned in their begging, than the other can do; and it is discovered more by his manner of speaking, his bemoaning himself. His pain and poverty makes him speak more in a spirit of lamentation than the other, and he is pitied sooner than the other, by all those that have the least dram of natural affection or pity. Just thus it is with God: there are some who out of custom and formality go and pray; there are others who go in the bitterness of their spirits: the one prays out of bare notion and naked knowledge; the other has his words forced from him by the anguish of his soul. Surely that is the man that God will look at, 'even to him that is poor, and of a contrite spirit, and trembleth at my word' (Is. 66. 2).

6. An understanding well enlightened is of admirable use also, both as to the matter and manner of prayer. He that has his understanding well exercised, to discern between good and evil, and in it a sense either of the misery of man, or the mercy of God, that soul has no need of the writings of other men to teach him by forms of prayer. For as he that feels the pain needs not to be taught to cry O! even so he that has his understanding opened by the Spirit needs not so to be taught of other men's prayers, as that he cannot pray without them. The present sense, feeling, and pressure that lies upon his spirit, provokes him to groan out his request unto the Lord. When David had the pains of hell catching hold on him, and the sorrows of hell compassing him about, he needs not a bishop in a surplice to teach him to say, 'O Lord, I beseech thee, deliver my soul' (Ps. 116. 3, 4). Or to look into a book, to teach him in a form to pour out his heart before God. It is the nature of the heart of sick men, in their pain and sickness, to vent itself for ease, by dolorous groans and complainings to them that stand by. Thus it was with David, in Ps. 38. 1–12. And thus, blessed be the Lord, it is with them that are endued with the grace of God.

7. It is necessary that there be an enlightened understanding, to the end that the soul be kept in a continuation of the duty of prayer.

The people of God are not ignorant how many wiles, tricks,

and temptations the devil has to make a poor soul, who is truly willing to have the Lord Jesus Christ, and that upon Christ's terms too, I say, to tempt that soul to be weary of seeking the face of God, and to think that God is not willing to have mercy on such a one as he. Ay, says Satan, you may pray indeed, but you will not prevail. Your heart is hard, cold, dull, and dead; you do not pray with the Spirit, you do not pray in good earnest, your thoughts are running after other things, when you pretend to pray to God. Away hypocrite, go no further, it is but in vain to strive any longer!

Here now, if the soul be not well informed in its understanding, it will presently cry out, 'The Lord hath forsaken me, and my Lord hath forgotten me' (Is. 49. 14). Whereas the soul rightly informed and enlightened says, Well, I will seek the Lord, and wait; I will not leave off, though the Lord keep silence, and speak not one word of comfort (Is. 40. 27). The Lord loved Jacob dearly, and yet he made him wrestle before he had the blessing (Gen. 32. 25–27). Seeming delays in God are no tokens of his displeasure; he may hide his face from his dearest saints (Is. 8. 17). He loves to keep his people praying, and to find them ever knocking at the gate of heaven; it may be, says the soul, the Lord tries me, or he loves to hear me groan out my condition before him.

The woman of Canaan would not take seeming denials for real ones; she knew the Lord was gracious, and the Lord will avenge his people, though he bear long with them (Luke 18. 1–6). The Lord has waited longer upon me than I have waited upon him; and thus it was with David, 'I waited patiently,' says he; that is, it was long before the Lord answered me, though at the last 'he inclined' his ear 'unto me, and heard my cry' (Ps. 40. 1). And the most excellent remedy for this is an understanding well informed and enlightened. Alas, how many poor souls are there in the world that truly fear the Lord, who, because they are not well informed in their understanding, are often ready to give up all for lost, upon almost every trick and temptation of Satan! The Lord pity them, and help them to 'pray with the Spirit, and with the understanding also.' Much of mine own experience could I here mention; when I have been in my fits of agonies of spirit, I have been strongly persuaded to leave off, and to seek the Lord no longer; but being made to understand what great sinners the Lord has had mercy upon, and how large his promises were still to sinners; and that it was not the whole, but the sick, not the righteous, but the sinner, not the full, but the empty, that he extended his grace and mercy unto—this made me, through the assistance of his Holy Spirit, to cleave to him, to hang upon him, and yet to cry, though for the present he made no answer. The Lord help all his poor, tempted, and afflicted people to do the like, and to continue, though it be long, according to the saying of the prophet (Hab. 2. 3). And the Lord help them (to that end) to pray, not by the inventions of men, and their stinted forms, but 'with the Spirit, and with the understanding also.'

4

QUERIES AND OBJECTIONS ANSWERED

First Query. But what would you have us poor creatures to do that cannot tell how to pray? The Lord knows I know not either how to pray, or what to pray for.

Answer. Poor heart! You complain that you cannot pray. Can you see your misery? Has God showed you that you are by nature under the curse of his law? If so, do not mistake, I know you groan and that most bitterly. I am persuaded you can scarcely be found doing any thing in your calling, but prayer breaks from your heart. Have not your groans gone up to heaven from every corner of your house? (Rom. 8. 26). I know it is thus; and so also does your own sorrowful heart witness your tears, and your forgetfulness of your calling. Is not your heart so full of desires after the things of another world that many times you even forget the things of this world? I pray you, read this Scripture: Job 23. 12.

Second Query. Yea, but when I go into a secret spot, and intend to pour out my soul before God, I can scarce say anything at all.

Answer. Ah! sweet soul! it is not your words that God so much regards, as if he would not regard you, unless you come before him with some eloquent oration. His eye is on the brokenness of your heart; and that it is that calls forth his

[43]

compassion. 'A broken and a contrite heart, O God, thou wilt not despise' (Ps. 51. 17).

The stopping of your words may arise from overmuch trouble in your heart. David was so troubled sometimes, that he could not speak (Ps. 77. 3, 4). But this may comfort all such sorrowful hearts as yours, that though you cannot through the anguish of your spirit speak much, yet the Holy Spirit stirs up in your heart groans and sighs, so much the more vehement: when the mouth is hindered, yet the spirit is not. Moses, as aforesaid, made heaven ring again with his prayers, although not one word came out of his mouth that we read of (Exod. 14. 15).

If you would more fully express yourself before the Lord, study, first, your fallen estate; secondly, God's promises; thirdly, the heart of Christ, which you may know or discern by his condescension and bloodshedding, also by mercy he has formerly extended to great sinners. Plead your own vileness, by way of bemoaning, Christ's blood by way of expostulation; and in your prayers, let the mercy that he has extended to other great sinners, together with his rich promises of grace, be much upon your heart. Yet let me counsel you to take heed that you content not yourself with words, and that you do not think that God looks only at words. However, whether your words be few or many, let your heart go with them; and then you shall seek him, and find him, when you seek him with your whole heart (Jer. 29. 13).

First objection. But though you have seemed to speak against any other way of praying but by the Spirit, yet here you yourself can give direction how to pray.

Answer. We ought to prompt one another to prayer, though we ought not to make forms of prayer for each other. To exhort to pray with Christian direction is one thing, and to make stinted forms for tying up the Spirit of God to them is another thing. The apostle gives Christians no form in which to pray, yet directs to prayer (Eph. 6. 8; Rom. 15. 30–32). Let no man therefore conclude, that because we may give instructions and directions to pray, therefore it is lawful to make forms of prayer for each other.

Second objection. But if we do not use forms of prayer, how shall we teach our children to pray?

Answer. My judgment is that men go the wrong way to teach their children to pray, in going about so soon to teach them any set form of words, as is commonly done.

For to me it seems to be a better way for people betimes to tell their children what cursed creatures they are, and how they are under the wrath of God by reason of original and actual sin; also to tell them of the nature of God's wrath, and the duration of the misery; which if they conscientiously do, they would sooner teach their children to pray than they do. Men learn to pray by conviction for sin, and this is the way to make our children do so too. But the other way, namely, to be busy in teaching children forms of prayer, before they know anything else, it is the way to make them cursed hypocrites, and to puff them up with pride. Teach therefore your children to know their wretched state and condition; tell them of hell-fire and their sins, of damnation, and salvation; the way to escape the one, and to enjoy the other, and this will bring tears to their eyes, and make hearty groans flow from their hearts; and then also you may tell them to whom they should pray, and through whom they should pray : you may tell them also of God's promises, and his former grace extended to sinners, according to the Word.

Ah! poor sweet babes, the Lord open their eyes, and make them holy Christians! Says David, 'Come, ye children, hearken unto me; I will teach you the fear of the Lord' (Ps. 34. 11). He does not say, I will muzzle you up in a form of prayer; but 'I will teach you the fear of the Lord;' which is, to see their sad state by nature, and to be instructed in the truth of the gospel, which through the Spirit begets prayer in every one that in truth learns it. And the more you teach them this, the more

[45]

will their hearts run out to God in prayer. God never did account Paul a praying man, until he was a convinced and converted man; no more will it be with any else (Acts 9. 11).

Third objection. But we find that the disciples desired that Christ would teach them to pray, as John also taught his disciples; and that thereupon he taught them that form called the Lord's Prayer.

Answer. To be taught by Christ, is that which not only they, but we desire; and seeing he is not here in his person to teach us, the Lord teaches us by his Word and Spirit; for the Spirit it is which he has said he would send to supply in his stead when he went away, and so it is (John 14. 16; 16. 7).

As to that called a form, I cannot think that Christ intended it as a stinted form of prayer. He himself lays it down diversely, as is to be seen, if you compare Matt. 6 with Luke 11. Whereas, if he intended it as a set form, it would not have been so laid down, for a set form is so many words and no more. We do not find that the apostles ever observed it as such; neither did they admonish others so to do. Search all their epistles; yet surely they, both for knowledge to discern, and faithfulness to practise, were as eminent as any of later date who would impose it.

But, in a word, Christ by those words, 'Our Father, &c.', instructs his people what rules they should observe in their prayers to God—that they should pray in faith—to God in the heavens—for such things as are according to his will, &c. Pray thus, or after this manner.

Fourth objection. But Christ bids men pray for the Spirit; this implies, that men without the Spirit may notwithstanding pray and be heard. See Luke 9. 9-13.

Answer. The Speech of Christ there is directed to his own, ver. 1. Christ's telling of them that God would give his Holy Spirit to them that ask him, is to be understood of giving more of the Holy Spirit; for still they are the disciples spoken to, which had a measure of the Spirit already; for he says, 'When ye pray, say, Our Father,' ver. 2. 'I say unto you,' ver. 8. And 'I say unto you,' ver. 9, 'If ye then, being evil, know how to give good gifts unto your children, how much more shall your heavenly Father give the Holy Spirit to them that ask him,' ver. 13. Christians ought to pray for the Spirit, that is, for more of the Spirit, though God has endued them with the Spirit already.

Question. Then would you have none pray but those that know they are disciples of Christ?

Answer. I answer:

1. Let every soul that would be saved pour out itself to God, though it cannot through temptation conclude itself a child of God.

2. I know if the grace of God be in you, it will be as natural to you to groan out your condition, as it is for a sucking child to cry for the breast. Prayer is one of the first things that discovers a man to be a Christian (Acts 9. 12). But yet if it be right, it is such prayer as follows. (1) To desire God in Christ, for himself, for his holiness, love, wisdom, and glory. For right prayer, as it runs only to God through Christ, so it centres in him, and in him alone. 'Whom have I in heaven but thee? And there is none upon earth that I desire,' long for, or seek after, 'beside thee' (Ps. 73. 25). (2) That the soul might enjoy continually communion with him, both here and hereafter. 'I shall be satisfied, when I awake with' thine image, or in 'thy likeness' (Ps. 17. 15). 'For in this we groan earnestly' (2 Cor. 5. 2). (3) Right prayer is accompanied with a continual labour after that which is prayed for. 'My soul waiteth for the Lord more than they that watch for the morning' (Ps. 130. 6). 'I will rise now, I will seek him whom my soul loveth' (Song of Sol. 3. 2). For mark, I beseech you, there are two things that provoke to prayer. The one is a detestation of sin and the things of this life; the other is a longing desire after communion with God in a holy and undefiled state and inheritance. Compare but this one thing with most of the prayers that are made by men, and you shall find them but mock prayers, and the breathings of an abominable spirit; for even the most of men either do not

5

USE AND APPLICATION

———

I shall now speak a word or two of application, and so conclude with, first, a word of information; second, a word of
encouragement; third, a word of rebuke.

(i) *A Word of Information*

As prayer is the duty of every one of the children of God, and
carried on by the Spirit of Christ in the soul, so every one that
takes it upon him to pray to the Lord, had need to be very
wary, and go about that work especially with the dread of God,
as well as with hopes of the mercy of God through Jesus Christ.

Prayer is an ordinance of God, in which a man draws very
near to God; and therefore it calls for so much the more of the
assistance of the grace of God to help a soul to pray as becomes
one that is in the divine presence. It is a shame for a man to
behave irreverently before a king, but a sin to do so before God.
And as a king, if wise, is not pleased with an oration made up
with unseemly words and gestures, so God takes no pleasure
in the sacrifice of fools (Eccles. 5. 1, 4). It is not long discourses,
nor eloquent tongues, that are the things which are pleasing in
the ears of the Lord, but a humble, broken, and contrite heart
(Ps. 51. 17; Is. 57. 15). Therefore for information, know that
there are these five things that are obstructions to prayer, and
even make void the requests of the creature.

1. When men regard iniquity in their hearts, at the time of
their prayers before God. 'If I regard iniquity in my heart, the
Lord will not hear' my prayer (Ps. 66. 18). There may be a secret

[49]

love to that very thing which you with your dissembling lips are judging against. For this is the wickedness of man's heart, that it will even love, and hold fast that which with the mouth it prays against: and of this sort are they that honour God with their mouth, but their heart is far from him (Is. 29. 13; Ezek. 33. 31). O how ugly it would be in our eyes, if we should see a beggar ask an alms, with an intention to throw it to the dogs! or that should say with one breath, Pray, bestow this upon me; and with the next, I beseech you, give it me not! And yet thus it is with this kind of person; with their mouth they say, 'Thy will be done;' but their hearts say no such thing. With their mouth they say, 'Hallowed be thy name,' and with their hearts and lives they delight to dishonour him all the day long. These be the prayers that become sin (Ps. 109. 7), and though they put them up often, yet the Lord will never answer them (2 Sam. 22. 42).

2. When men pray for show, to be heard, and thought somebody in religion, and the like; these prayers also fall short of God's approbation, and are never likely to be answered, in reference to eternal life. There are two sorts of men that pray to this end.

Showmanship

(1) Your trencher chaplains that thrust themselves into great men's families pretending the worship of God, when in truth the great business is their own bellies. These men were notably painted out by Ahab's prophets, and also Nebuchadnezzar's, who, though they pretended great devotion, yet their lusts and their bellies were the great things aimed at by them in all their pieces of devotion.

(2) Them also that seek repute and applause for their eloquent words, and seek more to tickle the ears and heads of their hearers than anything else. These be they that pray to be heard of men, and have all their reward already (Matt. 6. 5). These persons are discovered thus: (a) They eye only their auditory in their expressions. (b) They look for commendation when they have done. (c) Their hearts either rise or fall according to their praise or enlargement. (d) The length of their prayer pleases them; and that it might be long, they will vainly repeat

[50]

things over and over (Matt. 6. 7). They study for enlargements, but look not from what heart they come; they look for returns, but it is the windy applause of men. And therefore they love not to be in their chamber, but among company: and if at any time conscience thrusts them into their closet, yet hypocrisy will cause them to be heard in the streets; and when their mouths have done going their prayers are ended; for they wait not to hearken what the Lord will say (Ps. 85. 8).

3. A third sort of prayer that will not be accepted of God is, when either men pray for wrong things, or if for right things, yet that the thing prayed for might be spent upon their lusts, and laid out to wrong ends. Some have not, because they ask not, says James, and others ask and have not, because they ask amiss, that they may consume it on their lusts (Jas. 4. 2–4). If ends are contrary to God's will, it is a great argument with God to frustrate the petitions presented before him. Hence it is that so many pray for this and that, and yet receive it not. God answers them only with silence; they have their words for their labour, and that is all.

Objection. But God hears some persons, though their hearts be not right with him, as he did Israel, in giving quails, though they spent them on their lusts (Ps. 106. 14).

Answer. If he does, it is in judgment, not in mercy. He gave them their desire indeed, but they had better have been without it, for he 'sent leanness into their soul' (Ps. 106. 15). Woe be to that man that God answers thus!

4. Another sort of prayers there are that are not answered; and those are such as are made by men, and presented to God in their own persons only, without their appearing in the Lord Jesus. For though God has appointed prayer, and promised to hear the prayer of the creature, yet not the prayer of any creature that comes not in Christ. 'If ye shall ask anything in my name' (John 14. 13–14; 15. 16; 16. 23–26). And whether ye eat or drink, or whatsoever ye do, do all in the name of the Lord Jesus Christ (1 Cor. 10. 31). 'If ye shall ask anything in my name,' &c., though you be never so devout, zealous, earnest,

constant in prayer, yet it is only in Christ that you will be heard and accepted. But, alas! the most of men know not what it is to come to God in the name of our Lord Jesus, which is the reason they either live wicked, pray wicked, and also die wicked, or else that they attain to nothing but what a mere natural man may attain unto, as to be exact in word and deed betwixt man and man, and only with the righteousness of the law in which to appear before God.

5. The last thing that hinders prayer is, the form of it without the power. It is an easy thing for men to be very hot for such things as forms of prayer, as they are written in a book; but yet they are altogether forgetful to inquire with themselves whether they have the spirit and power of prayer. These men are like a painted man, and their prayers like a false voice. They in person appear as hypocrites, and their prayers are an abomination (Prov. 28. 9). When they say they have been pouring out their souls to God he says they have been howling like dogs (Hos. 7. 14).

When therefore you intend, or are minded to pray to the Lord of heaven and earth, consider seriously what you want. Do not as many, who in their words only beat the air, and ask for such things as indeed they do not desire, nor see that they stand in need thereof. When you see what you want, keep to that, and take heed you pray sensibly.

Objection. But I have a sense of nothing; then, by your argument, I must not pray at all.

Answer. 1. If you find yourself senseless in some sad measure, yet you cannot complain of that senselessness, for at least you have a sense of senselessness. According to your sense, then, that you have the need of anything, so pray; (Luke 8. 9), and if you are sensible of your senselessness, pray the Lord to make you sensible of whatever you find your heart senseless of. This was the usual practice of holy men of God. 'Lord, make me to know mine end' (Ps. 39. 4). 'Lord, open to us this parable,' said the disciples (Luke 8. 9). And to this is annexed the promise, 'Call unto me and I will answer thee, and show thee great and

[52]

mighty things which thou knowest not'—that is, that you are not sensible of. (Jer. 33. 3). *Jer 33.3*

Answer. 2. Take heed that your heart go to God as well as your mouth. Let not your mouth go any further than you strive to draw your heart along with it. David would lift his heart and soul to the Lord; and with good reason, for so far as a man's mouth goes along without his heart, so far it is but lip-labour only; and though God calls for, and accepts the calves of the lips, yet the lips without the heart argues, not only sense-lessness, but our being without sense of our senselessness; and therefore if you have a mind to enlarge in prayer before God, see that it be with your heart.

I shall conclude this use with a caution or two.

Caution 1. Take heed you do not throw off prayer, through sudden persuasions that you have not the Spirit, and that you do not pray thereby. It is the great work of the devil to do his best, or rather worst, against the best prayers. He will flatter your false dissembling hypocrites, and feed them with a thousand fancies of well-doing, when their very duties of prayer, and all other, stink in the nostrils of God, when at the same time he stands at a poor Joshua's hand to resist him, that is, to persuade him that neither his person nor performances are accepted of God (Is. 65. 5; Zech. 3. 1). Take heed, therefore, of such false conclusions and groundless discouragements; and though such persuasions do come in upon your spirit, be so far from being discouraged by them, that you use them to put yourself upon further sincerity and restlessness of spirit, in your approaching to God. *Resist* — *the devil's Temptation*

Caution 2. As such sudden temptations should not stop you from prayer, and pouring out your soul to God, so neither should your own heart's corruptions hinder you. It may be that you find in yourself all those things before mentioned, and that they endeavour to intrude themselves in your praying to him. Your business then is to judge them, to pray against them, and lay yourself so much the more at the foot of God, in a sense of your own vileness, and rather make an argument from your vileness and corruption of heart, to plead with God for justifying and sanctifying grace, than an argument of discouragement and despair. David went this way. 'O Lord,' said he, 'pardon mine iniquity, for it is great' (Ps. 25. 11).

(ii) *A Word of Encouragement*

I shall now speak a word by way of encouragement to the poor, tempted, and cast down soul, to pray to God through Christ. Though all prayer that is accepted of God in reference to eternal life must be in the Spirit—for that only makes intercession for us according to the will of God (Rom. 8. 29)—yet because many poor souls may have the Holy Spirit working on them, and stirring them up to groan unto the Lord for mercy, though through unbelief they do not, and, for the present, cannot believe that they are the people of God, such as he delights in; yet forasmuch as the truth of grace may be in them, I shall, to encourage them, lay down further these few particulars.

1. That scripture in Luke 11. 8, is very encouraging to any poor soul that hungers after Christ Jesus. The Lord first speaks a parable of a man that went to his friend to borrow three loaves, who, because he was in bed, denied him; yet for the sake of importunity, he did arise and give him, clearly signifying that though poor souls, through the weakness of their faith, cannot see that they are the friends of God, yet they should never leave off asking, seeking, and knocking at God's door for mercy. Mark, says Christ, 'I say unto you, though he will not rise and give him, because he is his friend; yet because of his importunity,' or restless desires, 'he will rise and give him as many as he needeth.' Poor heart! you cry out that God will not regard you, you do not find that you are a friend to him, but rather an enemy in your heart by wicked works (Col. 1. 21). And you are as though you hear the Lord saying to you, Trouble me not, I cannot give unto you, as said he in the parable; yet I say, continue knocking, crying, moaning, and bewailing yourself. I tell you Though he will not rise and give you, because you are his friend; yet, because of your importu-

nity, he will arise and give you as many as you need. The same in effect you have discovered in the parable of the unjust judge and the poor widow; her importunity prevailed with him (Luke 18). And verily, mine own experience tells me, that there is nothing that more prevails with God than importunity. Is it not so with you in respect of beggars that come to your door? Though you have no heart to give them anything at their first asking, yet if they follow you, bemoaning themselves, and will take no nay without an alms, you will give them; for their continual begging overcomes you. Is there compassion in you that are wicked, and will you be wrought upon by an importuning beggar? go then and do the like. It is a prevailing motive, and moved by experience, he will arise and give you as many as thou need (Luke 11. 8).

2. Another encouragement for a poor trembling convinced soul is to consider the place, throne, or seat, on which the great God has placed himself to hear the petitions and prayers of poor creatures; and that is a 'throne of grace' (Heb. 4. 16). 'The mercy-seat' (Exod. 25. 22). Which signifies, that in the days of the gospel God has taken up his seat, his abiding-place, in mercy and forgiveness; and from thence he intends to hear the sinner, and to commune with him, as he says in Exod. 25. 22—speaking before of the mercy-seat—'And there I will meet with thee'; mark, it is upon the mercy-seat : 'There I will meet with thee, and' there 'I will commune with thee, from above the mercy-seat.' Poor souls! They are very apt to entertain strange thoughts of God, and of his carriage towards them : and suddenly conclude that God will have no regard unto them, when yet he is upon the mercy-seat, and has taken up his place on purpose there, to the end he may hear and regard the prayers of poor creatures. If he had said, I will commune with thee from my throne of judgment, then indeed you might have trembled and fled from the face of the great and glorious Majesty. But when he says he will hear and commune with souls upon the throne of grace, or from the mercy-seat, this should encourage you, and cause you to hope, nay, to 'come

boldly unto the throne of grace, that you may obtain mercy, and find grace to help in time of need' (Heb. 4. 16).

3. There is yet another encouragement to continue in prayer with God : and it is this:

As there is a mercy-seat, from whence God is willing to commune with poor sinners, so there is also by this mercy-seat, Jesus Christ, who continually besprinkles it with his blood. Hence it is called 'the blood of sprinkling' (Heb. 12. 24). When the high-priest under the law was to go into the holiest, where the mercy-seat was, he might not go in 'without blood' (Heb. 9. 7).

Why so? Because, though God was upon the mercy-seat, yet he was perfectly just as well as merciful. Now the blood was to stop justice from being executed upon the persons concerned in the intercession of the high-priest, as in Lev. 16. 13–17; to signify, that all your unworthiness should not hinder you from coming to God in Christ for mercy. You cry out that you are vile, and therefore God will not regard your prayers. It is true, if you delight in your vileness, and come to God out of a mere pretence. But if from a sense of your vileness you pour out your heart to God, desiring to be saved from the guilt, and cleansed from the filth, with all your heart, fear not, your vileness will not cause the Lord to stop his ear from hearing. The value of the blood of Christ which is sprinkled upon the mercy-seat stops the course of justice, and opens a floodgate for the mercy of the Lord to be extended unto you. You have therefore, as aforesaid, 'boldness to enter into the holiest by the blood of Jesus,' that has made 'a new and living way' for you; you shall not die (Heb. 10. 19, 20).

Besides, Jesus is there, not only to sprinkle the mercy-seat with his blood, but he speaks, and his blood speaks; he has audience, and his blood has audience; insomuch that God says, when he does but see the blood, he 'will pass over you, and the plague shall not be upon you' (Exod. 12. 13).

I shall not detain you any longer. Be sober and humble; go to the Father in the name of the Son, and tell him your case, in the assistance of the Spirit, and you will then feel the benefit of praying with the Spirit and the understanding also.

(iii) *A Word of Reproof*

1. This speaks sadly to you who never pray at all. 'I will pray,' says the apostle, and so says the heart of them that are Christians. You then are not a Christian if you are not a praying person. The promise is that every one that is righteous shall pray (Ps. 32. 6). You then are a wicked wretch if you do not. Jacob got the name of Israel by wrestling with God (Gen. 32. 28). And all his children bear that name with him (Gal. 6. 16). But the people that forget prayer, that call not on the name of the Lord, they have prayer made for them, but it is such as this, 'Pour out thy fury upon the heathen,' O Lord, 'and upon the families that call not on thy name' (Jer. 10. 25). How like you this, O you that are so far off from pouring out your heart before God, that you go to bed like a dog, and rise like a hog, or a sot, and forget to call upon him? What will you do when you shall be damned in hell, because you could not find in your heart to ask for heaven? Who will grieve for your sorrow, that did not count mercy worth asking for? I tell you, the ravens and the dogs shall rise up in judgment against you, for they will, according to their kind, make signs, and a noise for something to refresh them when they want it; but you have not the heart to ask for heaven, though you must eternally perish in hell, if you have it not.

2. This rebukes you that make it your business to slight, mock at, and undervalue the Spirit, and prayer by the Spirit. What will you do when God shall come to reckon for these things? You count it high treason to speak but a word against the king, nay, you tremble at the thought of it; and yet in the meantime you will blaspheme the Spirit of the Lord. Is God indeed to be dallied with, and will the end be pleasant unto you? Did God send his Holy Spirit into the hearts of his people, to that end that you should taunt at it? Is this to serve God? and does this demonstrate the reformation of your church? nay, is it not the mark of implacable reprobates? O fearful!

Can you not be content to be damned for your sins against the law, but you must sin against the Holy Ghost?

Must the holy, harmless, and undefiled Spirit of grace, the nature of God, the promise of Christ, the Comforter of his children, that without which no man can do any service acceptable to the Father—must this, I say, be the burden of your song, to taunt, deride, and mock at? If God sent Korah and his company headlong to hell for speaking against Moses and Aaron, do you that mock at the Spirit of Christ think to escape unpunished? (Num. 16. 31–35; Heb. 10. 29). Did you never read what God did to Ananias and Sapphira for telling but one lie to the Holy Spirit? (Acts 5. 1–8). Also to Simon Magus for but undervalueing of the Spirit? (Acts 8. 18–22). And will your sin be a virtue, or go unrewarded with vengeance, that make it your business to rage against, and oppose the office, service, and help, that the Spirit gives to the children of God? It is a fearful thing to do despite unto the Spirit of grace (Matt. 12. 31; Mark 3. 30).

3. As this is the doom of those who openly blaspheme the Holy Ghost, in a way of disdain and reproach to his office and service : so also it is sad for you, who resist the Spirit of prayer by a form of man's inventing. It is a very juggle of the devil, that the traditions of men should be of better esteem, and more to be owned than the Spirit of prayer. What is this less than that accursed abomination of Jeroboam, which kept many from going to Jerusalem, the place and way of God's appointment to worship; and by that means brought such displeasure from God upon them, as to this day is not appeased 1 Kings 12. 26–33). One would think that God's judgments of old upon the hypocrites of that day should make them that have heard of such things take heed and fear to do so. Yet the leaders of our day are so far from taking of warning by the punishment of others, that they do most desperately rush into the same transgression, viz., to set up an institution of man, neither commanded nor commended of God; and whosoever will not obey herein, they must be driven either out of the land or the world.

Has God required these things at your hands? If he has, show us where? If not, as I am sure he has not, then what cursed presumption it is in any pope, bishop, or other, to command that in the worship of God which he has not required! Nay further, it is not that part only of the form, which is several texts of Scripture that we are commanded to say, but even all must be confessed as the divine worship of God, notwithstanding those absurdities contained therein, which because they are at large discovered by others, I omit the rehearsal of them. Again, though a man be willing to live never so peaceably, yet because he cannot, for conscience' sake, own that for one of the most eminent parts of God's worship, which he never commanded, therefore must that man be looked upon as factious, seditious, erroneous, heretical—a disparagement to the church, a seducer of the people, and what not? Lord, what will be the fruit of these things, when for the doctrine of God there is imposed, that is, more than taught, the traditions of men? Thus is the Spirit of prayer disowned, and the form imposed; the Spirit debased, and the form extolled; they that pray with the Spirit, though never so humble and holy, counted fanatics; and they that pray with the form, though with that only, counted the virtuous! And how will the favourers of such a practice answer that Scripture, which commands that the church should turn away from such as have 'a form of godliness, and deny the power thereof?' (2 Tim. 3. 5). And if I should say, that men do these things aforesaid, do advance a form of prayer of other men's making, above the spirit of prayer, it would not take long time to prove it. For he that advances the book of Common Prayer above the Spirit of prayer, he advances a form of men's making above it. But this do all those who banish, or desire to banish, them that pray with the Spirit of prayer; while they hug and embrace them that pray by that form only, and that because they do it. Therefore they love and advance the form of their own or others inventing, before the Spirit of prayer, which is God's special and gracious appointment.

Look into the jails in England, and into the alehouses of the same; and I trow you will find those that plead for the Spirit of prayer in the jail, and them that look only after the form

6

THE CONCLUSION

———

I shall conclude this discourse with this word of advice to all God's people.

1. Believe that as sure as you are in the way of God, you must meet with temptations.

2. The first day therefore that you enter into Christ's congregation, look for them.

3. When they do come, beg of God to carry you through them.

4. Be jealous of your own heart, that it deceive you not in your evidences for heaven, nor in your walking with God in this world.

5. Take heed of the flatteries of false brethren.

6. Keep in the life and power of truth.

7. Look most at the things which are not seen.

8. Take heed of little sins.

9. Keep the promise warm upon your heart.

10. Renew your acts of faith in the blood of Christ.

11. Consider the work of your generation.

12. Count to run with the foremost therein.
    Grace be with thee.

II

THE THRONE OF GRACE

'Let us therefore come boldly unto the throne of grace, that we may obtain mercy, and find grace to help in time of need'.

(Heb. 4. 16).

This epistle is indited and left to the church by the Holy Ghost, to show particularly, and more distinctly, the high priesthood of Jesus Christ, and the excellent benefits that his people have thereby; in which both the excellency of his person, and transcendent glory of his office, beyond either priest or priesthood of the law, is largely set forth before us.

Wherefore, in order to our beneficial reading of this epistle, the Spirit of God calls upon us, first, most seriously to consider how excellent this person is: 'Wherefore, holy brethren,' says he, you that are 'partakers of the heavenly calling,' consequently you that are related to and that are concerned in the undertaking of this Holy One, 'consider the Apostle and High priest of our profession, Christ Jesus' (Heb. 3. 1). Consider how great and how fit this man is for so holy and glorious a calling; He being so high, as to be far above all heavens; so great, as to be the Son of God, and God equal with the Father. Consider him also as to his humanity, how that he is really flesh of our flesh; sinlessly so, sympathisingly so, in all the compassions of a man; he is touched with, compassionates, pities, succours, and feels our infirmities, and makes our case his own. Nay, he again, from the consideration of his greatness and love, puts us upon a confident reliance on his undertaking, and also presses us to a bold approach to that throne of grace where he continually abides in the execution of his office: 'Seeing then,' says he, 'that we have a great high priest that is passed into the heavens, Jesus the Son of God, let us hold fast our profession. For we have not an high priest which cannot be touched with the feeling of our infirmities: but was in all points tempted like as

[65]

we are, yet without sin. Let us therefore come boldly unto the throne of grace' (Heb. 3. 14-16).

In the words we have, first, an exhortation; and second, an implication that we shall reap a worthy benefit, if we truly put the exhortation into practice. The exhortation is that we should come boldly to the throne of grace: 'Let us therefore come boldly unto the throne of grace.' In all we have an intimation of five things:

1. That God has more thrones than one; else the throne of grace need not to be specified by name. 'Let us come unto the throne of grace.'

2. That the godly can distinguish one throne from another. For the throne here is not set forth by where or what signs it should be known; it is only propounded to us by its name, and so left for saints to make their approach unto it: 'Let us come unto the throne of grace.'

3. The persons intended by this exhortation; 'Let us therefore come.' 'Us': What 'us'? or who are they that by this exhortation are called upon to come? 'Let us.'

4. The manner of the coming of these persons to this throne of grace; and that is through the veil, boldly, confidently: 'Let us come boldly unto the throne of grace.'

5. The motive to this exhortation; and that is twofold, first, because we have so great an high-priest, one that cannot but be touched with the feeling of our infirmities: 'Let us therefore come boldly unto the throne of grace.' And, second, because we are sure to speed: 'That we may obtain mercy, and find grace.'

I shall, as God shall help me, handle these things in order.

I

GOD HAS MORE THRONES THAN ONE

God has more thrones than one. He has a throne in heaven, and a throne on earth: 'The Lord's throne is in heaven,' and 'they shall call Jerusalem the throne of the Lord' Ps. 11. 4; Jer. 3. 17). He rules over the angels; he rules in his church. 'He ruleth in Jacob, unto the ends of the earth' (Ps. 59. 13). Yea, he has a throne and seat of majesty among the princes and great ones of the world. He rules or 'judgeth among the gods' (Ps. 82. 1). There is a throne for Him as Father, and a throne for Christ as a giver of reward to all faithful and overcoming Christians: 'To him that overcometh, will I grant to sit with me in my throne, even as I also overcame, and am set down with my Father in his throne' (Rev. 3. 21).

There is also to be a throne of judgment, on which God by Christ, at the great and notable day, shall sit to give to the whole world their last or final sentence; from which they shall never be released, no, not by any means. This throne is made mention of in the New Testament, and is called by Christ 'the throne of his glory,' and 'a great white throne' (Matt. 25. 31; Rev. 20. 11). And his presence, when he sits upon his throne, will be so terrible, that nothing shall be able to abide it that is not reconciled to God by him before.

Wherefore it is not amiss that I give you this hint, because it may tend to inform unwary Christians, when they go to God, that they address not themselves to him at rovers, or at random; but that when they come to him for benefits, they direct their prayer to the throne of grace, or to God as considered on a throne of grace. For he is not to be found a God merciful and gracious, but as he is on the throne of grace. This is his holy place, out of which he is terrible to the sons of men, and cannot be gracious unto them. For as when he shall sit at the last day upon his throne of judgment, he will neither be moved with the tears or misery of the world to do anything for them, that in the least will have a tendency to a relaxation of the least part of their sorrow; so now let men take him where they will, or consider him as they please, he gives no grace, no special grace, but as considered on the throne of grace: wherefore they that will pray, and speed, must come to the throne of grace: to a God that sits on the throne of grace: 'Let us therefore come boldly to the throne of grace, that we may obtain mercy.'

The unbeliever, the erroneous and superstitious, consider not this: wherefore they speak to God as their fancies lead them, not as the Word directs them, and therefore obtain nothing. Ask the carnal man to whom he prays; he will say, to God. Ask him where this God is; he will say, in heaven. But ask him how, or under what notion he is to be considered there, and he will give a few generals, but cannot direct his soul unto him as he is upon a throne of grace, as the apostle here bids, saying, 'Let us come boldly unto the throne of grace.' Wherefore they come and go, or rather go and come to no advantage at all: they find nothing but their labour or words for their pains. For the right considering of God when I go unto him, and how or where I may find him gracious and merciful, is everything; and mercy and grace is then obtained when we come to him as sitting upon a throne of grace.

2

THE GODLY CAN DISTINGUISH ONE
THRONE FROM ANOTHER

━━━

We come to the second thing, namely, that the godly can distinguish one throne from another. And the reason why I so conclude, is, as I said, because the throne here is not set forth unto us here, by where or what signs it should be known; it is only propounded to us by its name, a throne of grace, and so left for saints to make their approach thereto: 'Let us therefore come boldly unto the throne of grace.' We will consider the matter in its two parts: First, that there is a throne of grace. Second, that it is the privilege of the godly to distinguish this throne of grace from all other thrones whatsoever.

THERE IS A THRONE OF GRACE

This must be true, because the text says it; also it is that of which the mercy-seat, so often made mention of in the Old Testament, was a type, shadow, or figure; nor are the terms, seat and throne, of any strength to make this supposition void. For it is common for the antitype to be set forth in words more glorious than is the figure or shadow of that thing. And the reason is, that the heavenly things themselves are far more excellent than the shadow by which they are represented. What is a sheep, a bull, an ox, or calf, to Christ, or their blood to the blood of Christ? What is Jerusalem that stood in Canaan, to that new Jerusalem that shall come down from heaven? or the tabernacle made with corruptible things, to the body of Christ, or heaven itself? No marvel then, if they be set forth unto us by words of an inferior rank; the most full and aptest being reserved to set forth the highest things.

Before I proceed to give you a more particular description of this throne of grace, as also how it may be known, I will touch a little upon the terms themselves, and show briefly what must be implied by them.

Import of the term 'grace'

By this word grace, we are to understand God's free, sovereign, good pleasure, whereby he acts in Christ towards his people. Grace and mercy therefore are terms that have their distinct significations; mercy signifies pitifulness, or a running over of infinite compassion to objects in a miserable and help-less condition. But grace signifies that God still acts in this as a free agent, not being wrought upon by the misery of the creature, as a procuring cause; but of his own princely mind.

Were there no objects of pity among those that in the old world perished by the flood, or that in Sodom were burned with fire from heaven? Doubtless, according to our apprehension, there were many. But Noah, and he only, found grace in God's eyes; not because that of himself he was better than the rest, but God acted as a gracious prince towards him, and let him share in mercy of his own sovereign will and pleasure. But this at first was not so fully made manifest as it was afterwards. Wherefore the propitiatory was not called, as here, a throne of grace, but a mercy-seat. Yet there was great glory in this term also; for by mercy-seat was showed, not only that God had compassion for men, but that this was his continual resting-place, whither he would at length retire, and where he would sit down and abide, whatever terrible or troublesome work for his church was on the wheel [1] at present. For a seat is a place of rest, yea, is prepared for that end; and mercy is here called that seat, to show, as I said, that whatever work is on the wheel in the world, let it be never so dreadful and amazing, yet to God's church it shall end in mercy, for that is God's resting-place. Wherefore after God had so severely threatened and pun-

[1] An allusion to Jer. 18. 1–10.

ished his church under the name of a whorish woman, as you may read in the prophet Ezekiel, he says, 'So will I make my fury toward thee to rest, and my jealousy shall depart from thee; and I will be quiet, and will be no more angry.' And again, speaking of the same people and of the same punishments, he says, 'Nevertheless, I will remember my covenant with thee in the days of thy youth, and I will establish unto thee an everlasting covenant.' And again, 'I will establish my covenant with thee, and thou shalt know that I am the Lord; that thou mayest remember, and be confounded, and never open thy mouth any more because of thy shame, when I am pacified toward thee for all that thou hast done, saith the Lord God' (Ezek. 16. 42, 60–63). These, with many more places, show that mercy is God's place of rest, and thither he will retire at last, and from thence will bless his church, his people.

But yet the term 'throne', 'the throne of grace', does more exceed in glory : not only because the word grace shows that God, by all that he does towards us in saving and forgiving, acts freely as the highest Lord, and of his own good-will and pleasure, but also because he now says, that his grace is become a king, 'a throne of grace'. A throne is not only a seat for rest, but a place of dignity and authority. This is known to all. Wherefore by this word, a throne, or the throne of grace, is intimated, that God rules and governs by his grace. And this he can justly do : 'Grace reigns through righteousness, unto eternal life, through Jesus Christ our Lord' (Rom. 5. 21). So then, in that here is mention made of a throne of grace, it shows that sin, and Satan, and death, and hell, must needs be subdued. For these last mentioned are but weakness and destruction; but grace is life, and the absolute sovereign over all these to the ruling of them utterly down. A throne of grace!

But this then God plainly declares, that he is resolved this way to rule, and that he points at sin as his deadly foe : and if so, then, 'where sin abounds, grace must much more abound' (Rom. 5. 20). For it is the wisdom and discretion of all that rule, to fortify themselves against them that rebel against them. Wherefore he saith again, 'Sin shall not have dominion over you; for ye are not under the law, but under grace' (Rom. 6. 14). Sin seeks for the dominion, and grace seeks for the dominion; but sin shall not rule, because it has no throne in the church among the godly. Grace is king. Grace has the throne, and the people of God are not under the dominion of sin, but of the grace of God, the which they are here implicitly bid to acknowledge, in that they are bid to come boldly to it for help: 'That we may obtain mercy, and find grace to help; to help in time of need.' For as from the hand and power of the king comes help and succour to the subject, when assaulted by an enemy; so from the throne of grace, or from grace as it reigns, comes the help and health of God's people. Hence it is said again, 'A glorious high throne from the beginning is the place of our sanctuary' (Jer. 17. 12). Here then the saints take shelter from the roaring of the devil, from the raging of their lusts, and from the fury of the wicked. That also is a very notable word, 'He will subdue our iniquities; and thou wilt cast all their sins into the depths of the sea' (Micah 7. 19). He speaks here of God as solacing himself in mercy, and as delighting himself in the salvation of his people, and that without comparison: 'Who is a God like unto thee, that pardoneth iniquity, and passeth by the transgression of the remnant of his heritage? he retaineth not his anger for ever, because he delighteth in mercy' (Micah 7. 18). Thus have mercy and grace got into the throne to reign. They will assuredly conquer all; yea, will conquer, and that with a shout. 'Mercy rejoiceth against judgment' (Jas. 2. 13). Yea, mercy glories when it gets the victory over sin, and subdues the sinner unto God and to his own salvation, as is yet more fully showed in the parable of the prodigal son (Luke 15). But this, briefly to show you something of the nature of the terms, and what must necessarily be implied thereby.

What is to be inferred from the term 'throne of grace'?

We will in the next place show what is to be inferred from hence.

1. To be sure, this is inferred, that converted men are not every way, or in every sense, free from the being of sin. For,

were they, they need not betake themselves to a throne of grace for help. When it says there is grace in God, it infers that there is sin in the godly; and when it says grace reigns, as upon a throne, it implies that sin would ascend the throne, would reign, and would have the dominion over the children of God. This also is manifest, when he says, 'Let not sin therefore reign in your mortal body, that ye should obey it in the lusts thereof' (Rom. 6. 12). And the only way to prevent it is to apply ourselves, as by the text we are directed, to the throne of grace for help against it.

2. The text implies, that at certain times the most godly man in the world may be hard put to it by the sin that dwells in him; yea, so hard put to it, as that there can be no ways to save himself from a fall, but by imploring heaven and the throne of grace for help. This is called the needy time, the time when the wayfaring man that knocked at David's door shall knock at ours (2 Sam. 12); or when we are got into the sieve into which Satan did get Peter (Luke 22. 31); or when those fists are about our ears that were about Paul's; and when that thorn pricks us that Paul said was in his flesh (2 Cor. 12. 7, 8). But why, or how comes it to pass, that the godly are so hard put to it at these times? It is because there is in them, that is, in their flesh, no good thing, but consequently all aptness to close in with the devil and his suggestions, to the overthrow of the soul. But now here we are presented with a throne of grace, unto which, as David says, we must 'continually resort'; and that is the way to obtain relief, and to find help in time of need (Ps. 71. 3).

3. As Christians are sometimes in imminent danger of falling, so sometimes it is so, that they are fallen, are down, down dreadfully, and can by no means lift up themselves. And this happens unto them because they have been remiss as to the sincere performance of what by this exhortation they are enjoined to. They have not been constant supplicants at this throne for preserving grace; for had they, they should, as the text suggests, most certainly have kept from such a fall; help should have been granted them in their needful time. Such are guilty of

that which is written in the prophet Isaiah, 'But thou hast not called upon me, O Jacob; but thou hast been weary of me, O Israel' (Is. 43. 22). Therefore thou are profaned, therefore thou art given to reproaches (Is. 43. 28). Now, as they which are falling are kept from it by coming to this throne of grace, so those that are fallen must rise by the sceptre of love extended to them from thence. Men may fall by sin, but cannot raise up themselves without the help of grace. Wherefore, it is good for us to seek after a more thorough knowledge of this throne of grace, whence, as we may well perceive, our help comes, and whereby we are made to stand. I therefore come now to a more particular description of this throne of grace; and to show how the godly know, or may know it, from other thrones of God.

What this throne of grace is

This throne of grace is the humanity, or heart and soul of Jesus Christ, in which God sits and rests for ever in love towards them that believe in him. Forasmuch as Christ did, by the body of his flesh, when here, reconcile them unto the Father. 'The key of the house of David,' says God, 'will I lay upon his shoulder; so he shall open and none shall shut; and he shall shut and none shall open. And I will fasten him *as* a nail in a sure place; and he shall be for a glorious throne to his Father's house' (Is. 22. 22, 23). For a glorious throne to his Father's house, that is, for his Father's house, to come to their Father by; for that they shall always find him thereon; or, as another scripture saith, in Christ reconciling them unto God, not imputing to them their trespasses and sins (2 Cor. 5. 19). Nor is it possible, if we lay aside the human nature of Christ, for us to find any such thing as a throne of grace, either in earth or heaven; for then nothing can be found to be the rest of God. 'This is my beloved Son, in whom I am well pleased,' is God's own language; but there is none other of whom he has so said (Matt. 3. 17). Wherefore he rests in him towards us, and in him only. Besides, grace cannot be extended towards us but in a way of justice; for the law and our sin obstruct another way (Gen. 3. 24). But, lay the human nature of Christ aside, and where will you find THAT, that shall become such a sacrifice to justice for the sin of men, as that God, for the sake of it, shall both forgive, and cause that grace for ever should reign towards us in such a way? It reigns through righteousness, or justice, by Jesus Christ, and no way else. Christ Jesus, therefore, is this throne of grace, by which grace reigns towards the children of God (Rom. 5. 21).

That scripture also gives us a little light herein, 'And I beheld, and lo! in the midst of the throne . . . stood a Lamb, as it had been slain' (Rev. 5. 6). This is to show the cause why grace is so freely shown to us, even for that there stands there, in the midst of the throne, and in the midst of the elders, a Lamb as it had been slain, or, as it was made a sacrifice for our sin; for, as a slain Lamb, he now lives in the midst of the throne, and is the meritorious cause of all the grace that we enjoy. And though it seems by this text that the throne is one thing and the Lamb another, yet the Lamb of God is the throne, though not as a lamb or sacrifice, but as one that by his sacrifice has made way for grace to run like a river into the world. The Son of God, Jesus Christ, is ALL; he is the throne, the altar, the priest, the sacrifice, and all: but he is the throne, the priest, the altar, and the sacrifice, under divers considerations. He is not the throne as he is the priest; he is not the priest as he is the sacrifice; he is not the sacrifice as he is the altar; yet he is truly all these. Yet, there is no throne of grace, no high priest, no propitiatory sacrifice, but he; of all which we may yet speak further before we conclude this treatise. I conclude, then, that Christ Jesus, in his human nature, is this throne of grace. In his human nature, I say, he has completely accomplished all things necessary for the making way for grace to be extended to men. And that is not only God's place of rest, but by and from it, as upon a glorious throne, his grace shall reign over devil, death, sin, hell, and the grave, for ever. This human nature of Christ is also called the tabernacle of God, for the fulness of the Godhead dwells in it bodily. It is God's habitation, his dwelling-place, his chair and throne of state. He does all in and by it, and without it he does not anything. But we pass to the next thing.

Where the throne of grace is erected

We will now come to discourse of the placing of this throne of grace, or to discover where it is erected. And for this we must repair to the type, which, as was said before, is called the mercy-seat; the which we find, not in the outer court, nor yet within the first veil (Heb. 9. 3–5), which signifies, not in the world, nor in the church on earth, but in the holy of holies, or after the second veil, the flesh of Christ (Heb. 10. 20). There then is this throne of God, this throne of grace, and nowhere here below. And forasmuch as it is called the throne of God, of grace, and is there, it signifies that it is the highest and most honourable. Hence he is said to be far above all heavens, and to have a name above every name. Wherefore he that will come to this throne of grace, must know what manner of coming it is by which he must approach it; and that is, not personally,[1] but by runnings out of heart; not by himself, but by his Priest, his High-priest; for so it was in the type (Heb. 9. 7). Into the second, where the mercy-seat was, went the high-priest alone, that is, personally, and the people by him, as he made intercession for them. This then must be done by those that will approach this throne of grace. They must go to God, as he is enthroned *in* Christ; *by* Christ, as he is the High-priest of his church; and they must go to God in the Holiest, by him.

But again, as this throne of grace is in the Holiest, not in the world, not in the church on earth, so it is in this Holiest set up above the ark of the testimony; for so was the mercy-seat, it was set up in the most holy place, above the ark of the testimony (Deut. 10. 1–5; 1 Kings 8. 9; 2 Chron. 5. 10). The ark of the testimony! What was that? It was the place of the law, the ark in which it was kept: the testimony was the law, the ark was prepared to contain it. This ark in which was put this law

---

[1] Personally: used here with the sense of physically.

was set up in the Holiest, and the mercy-seat was set above it, for so was Moses commanded to place them. Thou shalt make an ark, said God, 'and thou shalt make a mercy-seat': the ark shall be called the ark of the testimony, and there 'thou shalt put the testimony that I shall give thee,' that is, the law, 'and thou shalt put the mercy-seat above upon the ark, and there I will meet with thee, from above the mercy-seat between the two cherubims, which are upon,' that is, above, 'the ark of the testimony,' 'shadowing the mercy-seat' (Exod. 25. 16–22; Heb. 9. 5).

Thus, then, were things of old ordained in the type, by which we gather what is now to be minded in our worshipping of God. There was an ark made, and the two tables of stone, in which the law was writ, were put therein (Deut. 10. 2–5). This ark, with these two tables, was put into the Holiest, and this mercy-seat was set above it. The Holy Ghost, in my mind, thus signifying, that grace sits upon a throne that is higher than the law, above the law; and that grace, therefore, is to rule before the law, and notwithstanding all the sentence of the law; for it sits, I say, upon a throne, but the law sits on none; a throne, I say, which the law, instead of accusing, justifies and approves. For although it condemns all men, yet it excepts Christ, who, in his manhood, is this throne of grace. Him, I say, it condemns not, but approves, and likes well of all his doings; yea, it grants him, as here we see, to be a throne of grace, and exalted above itself: yea, it cannot but so do, because by wisdom and holiness itself, which is also the Lord of the law, it is appointed so to do. Here, then, is the throne of God, the throne of grace, namely, above the ark of the testimony. On this God and his grace sits, reigns, and gives leave to sinners to approach his presence for grace and mercy. He gives, I say, for those sinners so to do, that have washed before in the brazen laver that is prepared to wash in first, of which we may speak more anon. Now, behold the wisdom of God in his thus ordaining of things; in his placing the law, and Christ the ark of the testimony, and the mercy-seat, or throne of grace, so nigh together; for doubtless it was wisdom that thus ordained them, and it might so ordain for these reasons:

Why the law and the mercy-seat are so near together

1. That we that approach the throne of grace might, when we come there, be made still to remember that we are sinners—'for by the law *is* the knowledge of sin' (Rom. 3. 20)—and behold just before us this ark in which are the two tables that condemn all flesh: yea, we must look that way, if we look at all, for just above it is the mercy-seat or throne of grace. So then here is a momento for them that come to God, and to his throne of grace, for mercy, namely, the law, by which they are afresh put in remembrance of themselves, their sins, and what need they have of fresh supplies of grace. I read that the laver of brass and its foot was made of the looking-glasses of the women that assembled at the door of the tabernacle (Exod. 38. 8), methinks to signify, that men might see their smyrches [1] when they came to wash. So here you see the law is placed even with, but beneath, the mercy-seat, whereby those that come to the throne of grace for mercy might also yet more be put in mind that they are sinners.

2. This also tends to set an edge upon prayer, and to make us the more fervent in spirit when we come to the throne of grace. Should a king ordain that the axe and halter should be before all those that supplicate him for mercy, it would put an edge upon all their petitions for his grace, and make them yet the more humbly and fervently implore his majesty for favour. But, behold, the mercy-seat stands above, is set up above the ark and testimony that is in it. Here, therefore, we have encouragement to look for good. For observe, though here is the law, and that too in the Holiest of all, whither we go; yet above it is the mercy-seat and throne of grace triumphant, unto which we should look, and to which we should direct our prayers. Let us therefore come boldly to the throne of grace, notwithstanding the ark and testimony is by; for the law cannot hurt us when grace is so nigh; besides, God is now not in

[1] Smutches or smudges.

the law, but upon the throne of grace that is above it, to give forth pardons, and grace, and helps at a time of need.

This, then, may serve to inform some whereabout they are, when they are in their closets, and at prayer. Are you most dejected when you are at prayer? Hear me, you are not far from the throne of grace; for your dejection proceeds from your looking into the ark, concerning which God has ordained that whosoever looks shall die (1 Sam. 6. 19). Now if you are indeed so near as to see your sins, by your reading of yourself by the tables in the ark, cast but up thine eyes a little higher, and behold, there is the mercy-seat and throne of grace to which you would come, and by which you must be saved. When David came to pray to God, he said he would direct his prayer to God, and would look up (Ps. 5. 3). As if he would say, When I pray, I will say to my prayers, O my prayers, mount up, stay not at the ark of the testimony, for there is the law and condemnation; but soar aloft to the throne that stands above, for there is God, and there is grace displayed, and there you may obtain what is necessary to help in time of need. Some, indeed, there be that know not what these things mean; they never read their sin nor condemnation for it when they are upon their knees at their devotion, and so are neither dejected at the sight of what they are, nor driven with sense of need to look higher for help; for need, indeed, they see none. Of such I shall say, they are not concerned in our text, nor can they come hither before they have been prepared so to do, as may appear before we come to an end.

HOW THE GODLY DISTINGUISH THE THRONE OF GRACE FROM OTHER THRONES

And now I come to show you how you shall find the throne of grace, and know when you are come to it.

First, then, *about the throne of grace there is a 'rainbow, in sight like unto an emerald'* (Rev. 4. 1–3). This was the first sight that John saw after he had received his epistles for the seven churches. Before he received them, he had the great vision of his Lord, and heard him say to him, I am he that was dead and am alive, or 'that liveth and was dead, and behold I am alive for evermore, Amen; and have the keys of hell and of death' (Rev. 1. 18). And a good preparation it was for a work of the nature that now he was called unto; namely, that he might the more warmly, and affectionately, and confidently attest the truth which his Lord had now for him to testify to them. So here, before he enters upon his prophecy of things to come, he hears a first voice, and sees a first sight. The first voice that he heard was, 'Come up hither,' and the first sight that he saw was a throne with a rainbow round about it. 'And immediately,' says he, 'I was in the Spirit; and behold a throne was set in heaven, and one sat on the throne. And he that sat was to look upon like a jasper, and a sardine stone, and there was a rainbow round about the throne' (Rev. 4. 1–3).

The first time that we find in God's Word mention made of a rainbow, we read also of its spiritual signification, namely, that it was a token of the firmness of the covenant that God made with Noah, as touching his not drowning the earth any more with the waters of a flood. 'I do set,' says he, 'my bow in the cloud, and it shall be for a token of a covenant between me and the earth. And it shall come to pass, when I bring a cloud over the earth, that the bow shall be seen in the cloud. And I will remember my covenant which is between me and you, and every living creature of all flesh: and the waters shall no more become a flood to destroy all flesh' (Gen. 9. 13–15). The first use, therefore, of the rainbow, was to be a token of a covenant of mercy and kindness to the world; but that was not the utmost end thereof. For that covenant was but a shadow of the covenant of grace which God has made with his elect in Christ, and that bow but a shadow of the token of the permanency and lastingness of that covenant. Wherefore the next time we read of the rainbow is in the first of Ezekiel, and there we read of it only with reference to the excellencies of its colour. It is there said to be exactly like the colour of the glory of the man that the prophet there saw as sitting upon a throne (v. 28). The glory, that is, the priestly robes; for he is a priest upon the throne, and his robes become his glory and beauty (Zech. 6. 13). His robes—what are they but his blessed righteousness, with the skirts of which he covers the sinful nakedness of his people, and with the perfection of which he decks and adorns them, 'as a bride adorneth herself with her jewels' (Exod. 28. 2; Ezek. 16. 8; Is. 61. 10).

Now here again, in the third place, we find a rainbow, a rainbow round about the throne; round about the throne of grace. A rainbow—that is, a token of the covenant, a token of the covenant of grace in its lastingness; and that token is the appearance of the man Christ. The appearance—that is, his robes, his righteousness, 'from the appearance of his loins even upward,' and 'from the appearance of his loins even downward' (Ezek. 1. 27); even down to the foot, as you have it in the book of the Revelation (1. 13). 'As the appearance of the bow that is in the cloud in the day of rain, so was the appearance of the brightness round about. This was the appearance of the likeness of the glory of the Lord (Ezek. 1. 28). The sum then is, that by the rainbow round about the throne of grace upon which God sits to hear and answer the petitions of his people, we are to understand the obediential righteousness of Jesus Christ, which in the days of his flesh he wrought out and accomplished for his people; by which God's justice is satisfied, and their persons justified, and they so made acceptable to him. This righteousness, that shines in God's eyes more glorious than the rainbow in the cloud does in ours, says John, is round about the throne. But for what purpose? Why, to be looked upon. But who must look upon it? Why, God and his people; the people when they come to pray, and God when he is about to hear and give. 'And the bow shall be in the cloud,' says God, 'and I will look upon it, that I may remember the everlasting covenant between God and every living creature of all flesh that is upon the earth' (Gen. 9. 16). And, I say, as the bow is for God to look on, so it is also for our sight to behold. A rainbow round about the throne, in sight; in whose sight? In John's and his companions', like unto an emerald.

We read of Solomon's great throne of ivory, that though

there was not its like in any kingdom, yet he was not willing that the bow of it should stand before him. It was round behind (1 Kings 10. 18–20). O! but God's throne has the bow before, even round about to view, to look upon in sight. Solomon's was but a shadow, and therefore fit to be put behind; but this is the sum and substance, and therefore fit to be before, in view, in sight, for God and his people to behold. Thus you see that a rainbow is round about the throne of grace, and what this rainbow is. Look then, when you go to prayer, for the throne; and that you may not be deceived with a fancy, look for the rainbow too. The rainbow, that is, as I have said, the personal performances of Christ your Saviour for you. Look, I say, for that, it is his righteousness; the token of the everlastingness of the covenant of grace; the object of God's delight, and must be the ground of the justification of thy person and performances before God. God looks at it, look you at it, and at it only (Ps. 71. 16). For in heaven or earth, if that be cast away, there is nothing to be found that can please God, or justify you. If it be said faith pleases God; I answer, faith is a relative grace; take then the relative away, which, as to justification, is this spangling robe, this rainbow, this righteousness of Christ, and faith dies, and becomes, as to what we now treat of, extinct and quenched as tow.

And a very fit emblem the rainbow is of the righteousness of Christ; and that in these particulars.

(1) The rainbow is an effect of the sun that shines in the firmament; and the righteousness by which this throne of grace is encompassed, is the work of the Son of God.

(2) The rainbow was a token that the wrath of God in sending the flood was appeased; this righteousness of Christ is that for the sake of which God forgives us all trespasses.

(3) The rainbow was set in the cloud, that the sinful man might look thereon, and wax confident in common mercy; this righteousness is showed us in the Word, that we may by it believe unto special mercy.

(4) The bow is seen but now and then in the cloud; Christ's righteousness is but here and there revealed in the Word.

[82]

(5) The bow is seen commonly upon, or after rain; Christ's righteousness is apprehended by faith upon, or soon after the apprehensions of wrath.

(6) The bow is seen sometimes more, sometimes less; and so is this righteousness, even according to the degree or clearness of the sight of faith.

(7) The bow is of that nature, as to make whatever you shall look upon through it, to be of the same colour as itself, whether that thing be bush, or man, or beast; and the righteousness of Christ is that that makes sinners, when God looks upon them through it, to look beautiful, and acceptable in his sight, for we are made comely through his comeliness, and made accepted in the Beloved (Ezek. 16. 14; Eph. 1. 6).

One word more of the rainbow, and then to some other things. As here you read that the rainbow is round about the throne; so if you read on even in the same place, you shall find the glorious effects thereof to be far more than all that I have said.

Secondly. As the throne of grace is known by the rainbow that is round about it; so also you may know it by this, *the high priest is continually ministering before it*; the high priest, or Christ as priest, is there before God in his high priest's robes, making continual intercession for your acceptance there. Now, as I said before, Christ is priest and throne and all; throne in one sense, priest in another; even as he was priest, and sacrifice, and altar too, when he became our reconciler to God.

As a priest here, he is described under the figure of an angel, of an angel that came and stood at the altar to offer incense for the church, all the time that the seven angels were to sound out with trumpets the alarm of God's wrath against the antichristian world; lest that wrath should swallow them up also. 'And,' says John, 'another angel came and stood at the altar, having a golden censer; and there was given unto him much incense, that he should offer it with the prayers of all saints upon the golden altar which was before the throne. And the smoke of the incense which came with the prayers of the

[83]

saints, ascended up before God out of the angel's hand' (Rev. 8. 1–4).

Here then you have before the throne, that is, the mercy-seat, the high priest; for there it was that God appointed that the altar of incense, or that to burn incense on, should be placed (Exod. 30. 1–7). This incense-altar in the type was to be overlaid with gold; but here the Holy Ghost implies, that it is all of gold. This throne then is the mercy-seat, or throne of grace, to which we are bid to come; and, as you see, here is the angel, the high priest with his golden censer, and his incense, ready to wait upon us. For so the text implies, for he is there to offer his incense with the prayers of all saints that are waiting without at his time of offering incense within (Luke 1. 10). So, then, at the throne of grace, or before it, stands the high priest of our propitiation, Christ Jesus, with his golden censer in his hand, full of incense, therewith to perfume the prayers of saints, that come thither for grace and mercy to help in time of need. And he stands there, as you see, under the name of an angel, for he is the angel of God's presence, and messenger of his covenant.

But now it is worth our considering how, or in what manner, the high priest under the law was to approach the incense-altar. When he came to make intercession for the saints before the throne, he was to go in thither to do this work in his robes and ornaments; not without them, lest he die. The principal of these ornaments were, 'a breast-plate, and an ephod, and a robe, and a broidered coat, a mitre, and a girdle' (Exod. 28. 4). These are briefly called his garments, in Revelation (Chapter 1), and in the general they show us that he is clothed with righteousness, and girded with truth and faithfulness, for that is the girdle of his reins to strengthen him (Is. 11. 5). Also he bears upon his heart the names of the children of Israel that are Israelites indeed; for as on Aaron's breast-plate were fixed the names of the twelve tribes of Israel, and he was to bear the weight of them by the strength of his shoulders, so are we on the heart of Christ (Is. 22. 21).

Thus therefore is our high priest within the Holiest to offer incense upon the golden altar of incense, that is, before the throne. Wherefore, when you go thither, even to 'the throne of grace', look for him, and be not content, though you should find God there, if you find Christ not there. I suppose now an impossibility, for edification's sake, for without Christ nothing can be done; I say, without him as a priest. He is the throne, and without him as a throne, God has no resting-place as to us; he is a priest, and without him as such we can make no acceptable approach to God; for by him as priest our spiritual sacrifices are accepted (1 Pet. 2. 5). 'By him, therefore, let us offer the sacrifice of praise to God continually, giving thanks,' and confessing to and 'in his name' (Heb. 13. 15). And for our further edification herein, let us consider, that as God has chosen and made him his throne of grace, so he has sworn, that he shall be accepted as a priest for ever there. As for his natural qualifications, we may speak something concerning them afterwards; in the meantime know that there is no coming to God, upon pain of death, without him.

Nor will it out of my mind, but that his wearing the rainbow upon his head does somewhat belong to him as priest, his priestly vestments being for glory and beauty, as afore was said, and compared to the colour of it (Rev. 10. 1; Ezek 1). But why does he wear the rainbow upon his head, but to show that the sign, that the everlastingness of the covenant of grace is only to be found in him. He wears it as a mitre or frontlet of gold, and can always plead it with acceptance to God, and for the subduing of the world and the good of his people.

Thirdly. The throne of grace is to be known by *the sacrifice that is presented there*. The high priest was not to go into the Holiest, nor come near the mercy-seat (the which, as I have showed you, was a type of our throne of grace) 'without blood.' 'But into the second went the high priest alone once every year, not without blood, which he offered for himself, and for the errors of the people' (Heb. 9. 7). Yea, the priest was to take of the blood of his sacrifice, and sprinkle it seven times before the Lord, that is, before the mercy-seat, or throne of grace; and was to put some of the blood upon the horns of the altar of incense

[85]

before the Lord (Lev. 4. 5–7; 16. 13–15). So then the throne of grace is known by the blood that is sprinkled thereon, and by the atonement that by it is made there. I told you before that before the throne of grace there is our high priest; and now I tell you, there is his sacrifice too; his sacrifice which he there presents as amends for the sins of all such as have a right to come with boldness to the throne of grace. Hence there is said to be in the midst of the throne, the same throne of which we have spoken before, 'a lamb as it had been slain' (Rev. 5. 6). The words are to the purpose, and signify that in the midst of the throne is our sacrifice, with the very marks of his death upon him; showing to God that sits upon the throne, the holes of the thorns, of the nails, of the spear; and how he was disfigured with blows and blood when at God's command he gave himself a ransom for his people; for it cannot be imagined that either the exaltation or glorification of the body of Jesus Christ should make him forget the day in which he died the death for our sins; specially since that which puts worth into his whole intercession is the death he died, and the blood he shed upon the cross, for our trespasses.

Besides, there is no sight more takes the heart of God, than to see of the travail of the soul, and the bruisings of the body of his Son for our transgressions. Hence it is said, He 'is in the midst of the throne' as he died, or as he had been slain (Rev. 7. 17). It is said again, 'The Lamb which is in the midst of the throne shall feed them.' The Lamb, that is, the Son of God as a sacrifice, shall be always in the midst of the throne to feed and comfort his people. He is the throne, he is the priest, he is the sacrifice. But then how as a Lamb is he in the midst of the throne? Why, the meaning in mine opinion is, that Christ, as a dying and bleeding sacrifice, shall be chief in the reconciling of us to God; or that his being offered for our sins shall be of great virtue when pleaded by him as priest, to the obtaining of grace, mercy, and glory for us (Heb. 9. 12). By his blood he enters into the holy place; by his blood he has made an atonement for us before the mercy-seat. His blood it is that speaks better for us than the blood of Abel did for Cain (Heb. 12. 24).

Also it is by his blood that we have bold admittance into the Holiest (Heb. 10. 19). Wherefore no marvel if you find him here a Lamb, as it had been slain, and that, in the midst of the throne of grace.

While you are therefore thinking on him, as he is the throne of grace, forget him not as he is priest and sacrifice; for as a priest he makes atonement. But there is no atonement made for sin without a sacrifice. Now, as Christ is a sacrifice, so he is to be considered as passive, or a sufferer. As he is a priest, so he is active, or one that has offered up himself. As he is an altar, so he is to be considered as God, for in and upon the power of his Godhead he offered up himself. The altar then was not the cross, as some have foolishly imagined. But as a throne, a throne of grace, he is to be considered as distinct from these three things, as I also have hinted before. Would you then know this throne of grace, where God sits to hear prayers and give grace? then cast the eyes of your soul about, and look till you find the Lamb there; a Lamb there 'as it had been slain,' for by this you shall know that you are right. A slain Lamb, or a Lamb as it had been slain, when it is seen by a supplicant in the midst of the throne, whither he is come for grace, is a blessed sight! A blessed sight indeed! And it informs him he is where he should be.

And you must look for this the rather, because without blood is no remission. He that thinks to find grace at God's hand, and yet enters not into the Holiest by the blood of Jesus, will find himself mistaken, and will find a dead, instead of 'a living way' (Heb. 10. 19). For if not anything below, or besides blood, can yield remission on God's part, how should remission be received by us without our acting faith therein? We are justified by his blood, through faith in his blood (Rom. 5. 6–9). Wherefore, I say, look when you approach the throne of grace, that you give diligence to look for the Lamb 'as it had been slain', in the midst of the throne of grace; and then you will have, not only a sign that you present your supplications to God where and as you should, but there also will you meet with matter to break, to soften, to bend, to bow, and to make your heart as you would have it. For if the blood of a goat will, as some say, dissolve an adamant, a stone that is harder than flint, shall not the sight of 'a Lamb as it had been slain' much more dissolve and melt down the spirit of the man that is upon his knees before the throne of grace for mercy, especially when he shall see, that not his prayers, not his tears, not his wants, but the blood of the Lamb, has prevailed with a God of grace to give mercy and grace to an undeserving man? This then is the third sign by which you shall know when you are at the throne of grace. That throne is sprinkled with blood; yea, in the midst of that throne there is to be seen to this day a Lamb as it had been slain; and he is in the midst of it, to feed those that come to that throne, and to lead them by and to 'living fountains of waters' (Rev. 7. 17). Wherefore,

Fourthly. The throne of grace is to be known, *by the streams of grace that continually proceed therefrom*, and that like a river run themselves out into the world. And, says John, 'He showed me a pure river of water of life, clear as crystal, proceeding out of the throne of God and of the Lamb' (Rev. 22. 1). Mark you, here is again a throne; the throne of God, which, as we have showed, is the human nature of his Son; out of which, as you read, proceeds a river, a river of water of life, clear as crystal. And the joining of the Lamb also here with God is to show that it comes, I say, from God, by the Lamb; by Christ, who as a lamb or sacrifice for sin, is the procuring cause of the running of this river; it proceeds out of the throne of God and of the Lamb. Behold, therefore, how carefully here the Lamb is brought in, as one from or through whom proceeds the water of life to us. God is the spring-head, Christ the golden pipe of conveyance, the elect the receivers of this water of life. He says not here, 'the throne of the Lamb', but 'and of the Lamb', to show, I say, that he it is out of or through whom this river of grace should come. But if it should be understood that it proceeds from the throne of the Lamb, it may be to show that Christ also has power as a mediator, to send grace like a river into the church. And then it amounts to this, that God, for

[88]

Christ's sake, gives this river of grace, and that Christ, for his merit's sake, has power to do so too. And hence is that good wish, so often mentioned in the epistles, 'Grace to you, and peace from God our Father, and the Lord Jesus Christ' (Rom. I. 7; I Cor. I. 3; 2 Cor. I. 2; Gal. I. 3; Eph. I. 2; Phil. I. 2; Col. I. 2; I Thess. I. 2; 2 Thess. I. 2; Philemon 3). And again, 'Grace, mercy, and peace, from God the Father and the Lord Jesus Christ (I Pet. I. 2; 2 Tim. I. 2; Tit. I. 4). For Christ has power with the Father to give grace and forgiveness of sins to men (John 5. 21–26; Mark 2. 10). But let us come to the terms in this text. Here we have a throne, a throne of grace; and to show that this throne is it indeed, there proceeds therefrom a river of this grace, put here under the term of 'water of life', a term fit to express both the nature of grace and the condition of him that comes for it to the throne of grace.

It is called by the name of water of life, to show what a reviving cordial the grace of God in Christ is, shall be, and will be found to be, by all those that by him shall drink thereof. It 'shall be in him', even in him that drinks it, 'a well of water springing up into everlasting life.' (John 4. 14). It will therefore beget life, and maintain it; yea, will itself be a spring of life, in the very heart of him that drinks it. Ah! it will be such a preservative also to spiritual health, as that by its virtue the soul shall for ever be kept, I say, the soul that drinks it, from total and final decay; it shall be in him a well of living water, springing up into everlasting life.

But there is also by this phrase or term briefly touched the present state of them that shall come hither to drink; they are not the healthful, but the sick. It is with the throne of grace, as it is with the waters of Bath, and other sovereign and healing waters; they are most coveted by them that are diseased, but do also show their virtues on those that have their health and limbs. So, I say, is the throne of grace; its waters are for healing, for soul-healing; that is their virtue (Ezek. 47. 8, 9). Wherefore, as at Nature's waters, the lame leave their crutches, and the sick such other tokens of their recovery as may be a sign of their receiving health and cure there, so at the throne of grace, true penitents, and those that are sick for mercy, do leave their sighs and tears; 'and the Lamb that is in the midst of the throne shall feed them, and shall lead them unto living fountains of waters; and God shall,' there, 'wipe away all tears from their eyes' (Rev. 7. 17). Wherefore, as Joseph washed his face, and dried his tears away, when he saw his brother Benjamin, so all God's saints shall here, even at the throne of grace, where is God's Benjamin, or the Son of his right hand, wash their souls from sorrow, and have their tears wiped from their eyes. Wherefore, O you that are diseased, afflicted, and that would live, come by Jesus to God as merciful and gracious; yea, look for this river when you are upon your knees before him, for by that you will find whereabout is the throne of grace, and so where you may find mercy.

But again, as that which proceeds out of this throne of grace is called 'water of life,' so it is said to be a river, a river of water of life. This, in the first place, shows, that with God is plenty of grace, even as in a river there is plenty of water. A pond, a pool, a cistern, will hold much, but a river will hold more. From this throne come rivers and streams of water of life, to satisfy those that come for life to the throne of God. Further, as by a river is showed what abundance of grace proceeds from God through Christ, so it shows the unsatiable thirst and desire of one that comes indeed aright to the throne of grace for mercy. Nothing but rivers will satisfy such a soul; ponds, pools, and cisterns, will do nothing: such an one is like him of whom it is said, 'Behold he drinketh up a river, and hasteth not; he trusteth that he can draw up Jordan into his mouth' (Job 40. 23). This David testifies when he says, 'As the hart panteth after the water-brooks, so panteth my soul after thee, O God' (Ps. 42. 1). Hence the invitation is proportionable, 'Drink abundantly' (Cant. 5. 1). They that are saved, are saved to receive abundance of grace; 'they which receive abundance of grace, and of the gift of righteousness, shall reign in life by one, Jesus Christ' (Rom. 5. 17). And hence it is said again, 'When the poor and needy seek water, and there is none, and their tongue faileth for thirst, I the Lord will hear them, I the

God of Israel will not forsake them' (Is. 41. 17). But, Lord, how wilt thou quench their boundless thirst? 'I will open rivers in high places, and fountains in the midst of the valleys: I will make the wilderness a pool of water, and the dry land springs of water' (Is. 41. 17, 18). Behold, here is a pool of water as big as a wilderness, enough one would think to satisfy any thirsty soul. O, but that will not do! Wherefore he will open rivers, fountains, and springs, and all this to quench the drought of one that thirsts for the grace of God, until he has enough. 'They shall be abundantly satisfied with the fatness of thy house, and thou shalt make them drink of the river of thy pleasures, for with thee is the fountain of life' (Ps. 36. 8, 9).

This abundance the throne of grace yields for the help and health of such as would have the water of life to drink, and to cure their diseases withal: it yields a river of water of life. Moreover, since grace is said here to proceed as a river from the throne of God and of the Lamb, it is to show the commonness of it; rivers you know are common in the stream, however they are at the head. And to show the commonness of it, the apostle calls it 'the common salvation' (Jude 3); and it is said in Ezekiel and Zechariah, to go forth to the desert, and into the sea, the world, to heal the beasts and fish of all kinds that are there (Ezek. 47. 8; Zech. 14. 8). This, therefore, is a text that shows us what it is to come to a throne, where the token of the covenant of grace is, where the high priest ministers, and in the midst of which there is a Lamb, 'as it had been slain': for from thence there come not drops, nor showers, but rivers of the grace of God, a river of water of life.

Again, as the grace that we here read of is said, as it comes from this throne, to come as a river of water of life, so it is said to be pure and clear as crystal. 'Pure' is set in opposition to muddy and dirty waters, and 'clear' is set in opposition to those waters that are black, by reason of their cold and icyish nature; therefore there is conjoined to this phrase the word 'crystal', which all know is a clear and shining stone (Ezek. 34. 19; Job 6. 15, 16). Indeed the life and spirit that is in this water will keep it from looking black and dull; and the throne from whence it comes will keep it from being muddy, so much as in the streams thereof. 'The blessing of the Lord, it maketh rich, and he addeth no sorrow with it' (Prov. 10. 22). Indeed, all the sorrow that is mixed with our Christianity proceeds, as the procuring cause, from ourselves, not from the throne of grace; for that is the place where our tears are wiped away, and also where we hang up our crutches. The streams thereof are pure and clear, not muddy nor frozen, but warm and delightful, and they 'make glad the city of God' (Ps. 46. 4).

These words also show us, that this water of itself can do without a mixture of anything of ours. What comes from this throne of grace is pure grace, and nothing else; clear grace, free grace, grace that is not mixed, nor need be mixed with works of righteousness which we have done; it is of itself sufficient to answer all our wants, to heal all our diseases, and to help us at a time of need. It is grace that chooses, it is grace that calls, it is grace that preserves, and it is grace that brings to glory: even the grace that like a river of water of life proceeds from this throne. And hence it is that, from first to last, we must cry, 'Grace, grace unto it!' (Zech. 4. 7).

Thus you see what a throne the Christian is invited to; it is a throne of grace whereon sits the God of all grace; it is a throne of grace before which the Lord Jesus ministers continually for us; it is a throne of grace sprinkled with the blood, and in the midst of which is a Lamb as it had been slain; it is a throne with a rainbow round about it, which is the token of the everlasting covenant, and out of which proceeds, as here you read, a river, a pure river of water of life, clear as crystal. Look then for these signs of the throne of grace, all you that would come to it, and rest not, until by some of them you know that you are even come to it; they are all to be seen have you but eyes. The sight of them is very delectable, and they have a natural tendency in them, when seen, to revive and quicken the soul.

Fifthly. As the throne of grace is known and distinguished by the things above named, *so it is also by the effects which these things have wrought*. There are about that throne 'four and twenty seats, and upon the seats four and twenty elders sitting, clothed in white raiment, and . . . on their heads crowns of gold' (Rev. 4. 4). There is no throne that has these signs and effects belonging to it but this; wherefore, as by these signs, so by the effects of them also, one may know which is, and so when he is indeed come to, the throne of grace. And a little as we commented upon what went before, we will also touch upon this.

1. By seats, I understand places of rest and dignity; places of rest, for they that sit on them do rest from their labours; and places of dignity, for they are about the throne (Rev. 14. 13). 'And the four and twenty elders which sat before God on their seats, fell upon their faces and worshipped God' (Rev. 11. 16). And forasmuch as the seats are mentioned, before they are mentioned that sat thereon, it is to show, that the places were prepared before they were converted.

2. The elders, I take to be the twelve patriarchs and the twelve apostles, or the first fathers of the churches; for they are the elders of both the churches, that is, both of the Jewish and Gentile church of God; they are the ancients, as also they are called in the prophet Isaiah, which are in some sense the fathers of both these churches (Is. 24. 23). These elders are well set forth by that four and twenty that you read of in the book of Chronicles, who had every one of them for sons twelve in number. There therefore the four and twenty are (1 Chron. 25. 8–31).

3. Their sitting denotes also their abiding in the presence of God. 'Sit thou at my right hand,' was the Father's word to the Son, and also signifies the same (Ps. 110. 1). It is then the throne of grace where the four and twenty seats are, and before which the four and twenty elders sit.

4. Their white robes are Christ's righteousness, their own good works and glory; not that their works brought them thither, for they were of themselves polluted, and were washed white in the blood of the Lamb; but yet God will have all that his people have done in love to him to be rewarded. Yea, and

they shall wear their own labours, being washed as afore is hinted, as a badge of their honour before the throne of grace, and this is grace indeed. 'They have washed their robes, and made them white in the blood of the Lamb; therefore are they before the throne of God' (Rev. 7. 14, 15). They have washed as others did before them.

5. 'And they had on their heads crowns of gold' (Rev. 4. 4). This denotes their victory, and also that they are kings, and as kings shall reign with him for ever and ever' (Rev. 5. 10).

6. But what! were they silent? did they say, did they do nothing while they sat before the throne? Note, they were appointed to be singers there. This was signified by the four and twenty that we made mention of before, who with their sons were instructed in the songs of the Lord, and all that were cunning to do so then, were two hundred fourscore and eight (1 Chron. 25. 7). These were the figure of that hundred and forty four thousand redeemed from the earth. For as the first four and twenty, and their sons, are said to sing and to play upon cymbals, psalteries, and harps; and as they are there said to be instructed and cunning in the songs of the Lord; so these that sit before the throne are said also to sing with harps in their hands their song before the throne; and such song it was, and so cunningly did they sing it, that 'no man could learn it, but the hundred and forty and four thousand which were redeemed from the earth' (Rev. 14. 3).

Now, as I said, as he at first began with four and twenty in David, and ended with four and twenty times twelve, so here in John he begins with the same number, but ends with such a company that no man could number. For, he says, 'After this I beheld, and lo, a great multitude which no man could number, of all nations, and kindreds, and people, and tongues stood before the throne, and before the Lamb, clothed with white robes, and palms in their hands. And cried with a loud voice, saying, Salvation to our God, which sitteth upon the throne, and unto the Lamb. And all the angels stood round about the throne, and the elders, and the four beasts, and fell before the throne on their faces, and worshipped God' (Rev.

7. 9–11). This numberless number seems to have got hold of the song by the end, for they cry aloud, 'Salvation, salvation to our God and to the Lamb'; which to be sure is such a song that none can learn but them that are redeemed from the earth.

But I say, what a brave encouragement it is for one that is come for grace to the throne of grace, to see so great a number already there, on their seats, in their robes, with their palms in their hands, and their crowns upon their heads, singing of salvation to God and to the Lamb! And I say again, and speak now to the dejected, methinks it would be strange, O you that are so afraid that the greatness of your sins will be a bar unto you, if amongst all this great number of pipers and harpers that are got to glory, you cannot espy one that when here was as vile a sinner as yourself. Look man, they are there for you to view them, and for you to take encouragement to hope, when you consider what grace and mercy has done for them. Look again, I say, now you are upon your knees, and see if some that are among them have not done worse than you have done. And yet behold, they are set down; and yet behold they have their crowns on their heads, their harps in their hands, and sing aloud of salvation to their God, and to the Lamb.

This then is a fifth note or sign that distinguishes the throne of grace from other thrones. There are, before that throne, to be seen, for our encouragement, a numberless number of people sitting and singing round about it. Singing, I say, to God for his grace, and to the Lamb for his blood, by which they are secured from the wrath to come. 'And the four and twenty elders fell down before the Lamb, having every one of them harps, and golden vials full of odours, which are the prayers of saints. And they sung a new song, saying, Thou art worthy to take the book, and to open the seals thereof; for thou wast slain, and hast redeemed us to God by thy blood, out of every kindred, and tongue, and people, and nation; and hast made us unto our God kings and priests, and we shall reign on the earth' (Rev. 5. 8–10). Behold, tempted soul, do you not yet see what a throne of grace is here, and what multitudes are already arrived thither, to give thanks unto his name that sits thereon, and to the Lamb for ever and ever? And will you hang your harp upon the willows, and go drooping up and down the world, as if there was no God, no grace, no throne of grace, to apply yourself unto, for mercy and grace to help in time of need? Hark! do you not hear them what they say, 'Worthy,' say they, 'is the Lamb that was slain, to receive power, and riches, and wisdom, and strength, and honour, and glory, and blessing. And every creature which is in heaven,' where they are, 'and on the earth,' where you are, 'and under the earth, and such as are in the sea, and all that are in them, heard I saying, Blessing, and honour, and glory, and power *be* unto him that sitteth upon the throne, and unto the Lamb for ever and ever' (Rev. 5. 12, 13).

All this is written for our learning, that we through patience and comfort of the Scriptures might have hope; and that the drooping ones might come boldly to the throne of grace, to obtain mercy and find grace to help in time of need. They bless, they all bless; they thank, they all thank; and will you hold your tongue? 'They have all received of his fulness, and grace for grace' (John 1. 16); and will he shut you out? Or is his grace so far gone, and so near spent, that now he has not enough to pardon, and secure, and save one sinner more? For shame, leave off this unbelief! Wherefore, do you think, are you told of all this, but to encourage you to come to the throne of grace? And will you hang back or be sullen, because you are none of the first? since he hath said, 'The first shall be last, and the last first' (Matt. 19. 30). Behold the legions, the thousands, the untold and numberless number that stand before the throne, and be bold to hope in his mercy.

Sixthly. The throne of grace is known *by what proceeds from it.* As the throne of grace is distinguished from other thrones by these, so 'out of this throne proceed lightnings, and thunderings, and voices.' Also before this throne are 'seven lamps of fire burning, which are the seven spirits of God' (Rev. 4. 5). This then is another thing by which the throne of grace may be known. And again, it is said, that from the altar of incense that stood before the throne, 'there were voices, and thunderings, and lightnings, and an earthquake' (Rev. 8. 5). All these then come out of the Holiest, where the throne is, and are inflamed by this throne, and by him that sits thereon.

1. Lightnings here are to be taken for the illuminations of the Spirit in the gospel (Heb. 10. 32). As it is said in the book of Psalms, 'They looked unto him,' on the throne, 'and were lightened' (Ps. 34. 5). Or, as it is said in other places, 'The voice of thy thunder was in the heaven, the lightnings lightened the world' (Ps. 77. 18). And again, 'His lightnings enlightened the world, the earth saw and trembled' (Ps. 97. 4). This lightning therefore communicates light to them that sit in darkness. 'God,' says the apostle, 'who commanded the light to shine out of darkness, hath shined in our hearts, to give the light of the knowledge of the glory of God in the face of Jesus Christ' (2 Cor. 4. 6). It was from this throne that the light came that struck Paul off his horse, when he went to destroy it and the people that professed it (Acts 9. 3). These are those lightnings by which sinners are made to see their sad condition, and by which they are made to see the way out of it. Are you then made to see your condition, how bad it is, and that the way out of it is by Jesus Christ? for, as I said, he is the throne of grace. Why then, come orderly in the light of these convictions to the throne from whence your light did come, and cry there, as Samuel did to Eli, 'Here am I, for thou hast called me' (I Sam. 3. 8). Thus did Saul by the light that made him see; by it he came to Christ, and cried, 'Who art thou, Lord?' and, 'What wilt thou have me to do?' (Acts 9. 5–6). And is it not an encouragement to you to come to him, when he lights your candle that you might see the way; yea, when he does it on purpose that you might come to him? 'He gives light to them that sit in darkness, and in the shadow of death'; what to do? 'To guide our feet into the way of peace' (Luke 1. 79). This interpretation of this place seems to me to cohere with what went before; for first you have here a throne, and one sitting on it; then you have the elders, and in them presented to you the whole church, sitting round about the throne; then you

have in the words last read unto you, a discourse how they came thither, and that is, by the lightnings, thunderings, and voices that proceed out of the throne.

2. As you have here lightnings, so thereto is adjoined thunders. There proceeded out of this throne lightnings and thunders. By thunders, I understand that powerful discovery of the majesty of God by the Word of truth, which seizes the heart with a reverential dread and awe of him : hence it is said, 'The voice of the Lord is full of majesty; the voice of the Lord breaketh the cedars' (Ps. 29. 45). The voice, that is, his thundering voice. 'Canst thou thunder with a voice like him?' (Job 40. 9). And 'the thunder of his power who can understand?' (Job 26. 14). It was upon this account that Peter, and James, and John, were called 'the sons of thunder,' because, in the word which they were to preach, there was to be not only lightnings, but thunders; not only illuminations, but a great seizing of the heart, with the dread and majesty of God, to the effectual turning of the sinner to him (Mark 3. 16, 17).

Lightnings without thunder are in this case dangerous, because they that receive the one without the other are liable to miscarry. They were 'once enlightened,' but you read of no thunder they had; and they were liable to fall into an irrecoverable state (Heb. 6. 4–6). Saul had thunder with his lightnings to the shaking of his soul; so had the three thousand; so had the jailor (Acts 2. 9, 16). They that receive light without thunder are liable to turn the grace of God into wantonness; but they that know the terror of God will persuade men (Rom. 3. 8; Jude 4; 2 Cor. 5. 11). So then, when he decrees to give the rain of his grace to a man, he makes 'a way for the lightning of the thunder'; not the one without the other, but the one following the other (Job. 28. 26). Lightning and thunder is made a cause of rain, but lightning alone is not: 'Who hath divided a water-course for the overflowing of waters? or a way for the lightning of thunder to cause it to rain on the earth, where no man is: on the wilderness wherein there is no man?' (Job 38. 25, 26).

Thus you may see how in the darkest sayings of the Holy

Ghost there is as great an harmony with truth as in the most plain and easy; there must be thunder with light, if your heart be well poised and balanced with the fear of God : we have had great lightnings in this land of late years, but little thunders; and that is one reason why so little grace is found where light is, and why so many professors run on their heads in such a day as this is, notwithstanding all they have seen. Well then, this also should be a help to a soul to come to the throne of grace; the God of glory has thundered, has thundered to awaken you, as well as sent lightnings to give you light; to awaken you to a coming to him, as well as to enable you to see his things; this then has come from the throne of grace to make you come hither : wherefore come to the throne of grace.

3. As there proceed from this throne lightnings and thunders, so from hence it is said voices proceed also : now these voices may be taken for such as are sent with this lighting and thunder to instruct, or for such as this lightning and thunder begets in our hearts.

It may be taken in the first sense for light and dread, when it falls from God into the soul, and is attended with a voice or voices of instruction to the soul, to know what to do (Acts 2. 3–7). Thus it was in Paul's case. He had light and dread, and voices for his instruction; he had lightnings, and thunderings, and voices. 'Good and upright is the Lord; therefore will he teach sinners in the way. The meek will he guide in judgment; and the meek will he teach his way' (Ps. 25. 8, 9).

Or by voices you may understand, such as the lightning and thunder begets in our hearts : for though man is as mute as a fish to Godward, before this thunder and lightning comes to him, yet after that he is full of voices (2 Cor. 4. 13; 7. 14). And how much more numerous are the voices that in the whole church on earth are begotten by these lightnings and thunders that proceed from the throne of grace. Their faith has a voice, their repentance has a voice, their subjection to God's Word has a voice in it; yea, there is a voice in their prayers, a voice in their cries, a voice in their tears, a voice in their groans, in their roarings, in their bemoaning of themselves, and in their

3

THE PERSONS INTENDED BY THE
EXHORTATION 'LET US COME'

Now the persons here called upon to come to the throne of grace, are not all or every sort of men, but the men that may properly be comprehended under the words Us and We; 'let Us therefore come boldly, that We may obtain.' And they that are here put under these particular terms, are expressed both before and after.

They are called (in the epistle to the Hebrews), such as give the more earnest heed to the word which they have heard. They are such as see Jesus crowned with glory and honour. They are called the children. They are called the seed of Abraham. They are called Christ's brethren (Heb. 2. 1, 9, 14, 16, 17).

So, in the third chapter, they are called holy brethren, and said to be partakers of the heavenly calling, and the people of whom it is said that Christ Jesus is the apostle and high priest of their profession (Heb. 3. 1–6). They are called Christ's own house, and are said to be partakers of Christ (Heb. 3. 14). They are said to be believers, those that enter into rest, those that have Christ for a high priest, and with the feeling of whose infirmities he is touched and sympathises (Heb. 4. 3, 14, 15).

So, in chapter six, they are called beloved, and the heirs of promise; they that have fled for refuge to lay hold on the hope set before them. They are called those that have hope as an anchor, and those for whom Christ as a forerunner has entered and taken possession of Heaven (Heb. 6. 9, 17–20). So in the seventh chapter, they are said to be such as draw nigh unto God (Heb. 7. 19). And in chapter eight they are said to be such with whom the new covenant is made in Christ. In the ninth chapter, they are such for whom Christ has obtained eternal redemption, and such for whom he has entered the holy place (Heb. 9. 12, 22). In chapter ten, they are such as are said to be sanctified by the will of God, such as have boldness to enter into the Holiest by the blood of Jesus; such as draw near with a true heart, in full assurance of faith, or that have liberty to do so, having their hearts sprinkled from an evil conscience, and their bodies washed with pure water; they were those that had suffered much for Christ in the world, and that became companions of them that were so used (Heb. 10. 10, 19, 22–25). Yea, he tells them, in the eleventh chapter, that they and the patriarchs must be made perfect together (Heb. 11. 40). He also tells them, in the twelfth chapter, that already they are 'come to Mount Zion, to the city of the living God, the heavenly Jerusalem, and to an innumerable company of angels; to the general assembly and church of the first born which are written in Heaven, and to God the Judge of all; and to the spirits of just men made perfect, and to Jesus the mediator of the New Testament, and to the blood of sprinkling, that speaketh better things than that of Abel' (Heb. 12. 22–24).

Thus you see what terms, characters, titles, and privileges they are invested with that are here exhorted to come to the throne of grace. From whence we may conclude that every one is not capable of coming thither, no not every one that is under convictions, and that has a sense of the need of and a desire after the mercy of God in Christ.

The orderly coming to the throne of grace

Wherefore we will come, in the next place, to show the orderly coming of a soul to the throne of grace for mercy: and for this we must first apply ourselves to the Old Testament, where we have the shadow of what we now are about to enter upon the discourse of, and then we will come to the antitype, where yet the thing is far more explained.

The mercy-seat was for the church, not for the world; for a Gentile could not go immediately from his natural state to the mercy-seat, by the high priest, but must first orderly join himself, or be joined, to the church, which then consisted of the body of the Jews (Exod. 12. 43–49). The stranger then must first be circumcised, and consequently profess faith in the Messiah to come, which was signified by his going from his circumcision directly to the passover, and so orderly to other privileges, specially to this of the mercy-seat which the high-priest was to go but once a year to (Ezek. 44. 6–9).

The church is again set forth unto us by Aaron and his sons; Aaron as the head, his sons as the members. But the sons of Aaron were not to meddle with any of the things of the Holiest, until they had washed in a laver: 'And the Lord spake unto Moses, saying, Thou shalt also make a laver of brass, and his foot also of brass, to wash in; and thou shalt put it between the tabernacle of the congregation and the altar, and thou shalt put water therein. For Aaron and his sons shall wash their hands and their feet thereat. When they go into the tabernacle of the congregation they shall wash with water, that they die not; or when they come near to the altar to minister, to burn offerings made by fire unto the Lord. So they shall wash their hands and their feet that they die not; and it shall be a statute for ever unto them, even to him, and to his seed throughout their generations' (Exod. 30. 17–21; 40. 30–32).

Nay, so strict was this law, that if any of Israel, as well as the stranger, were defiled by any dead thing, they were to wash before they partook of the holy things, or else to abstain: but if they did not, their sin should remain upon them (Lev. 17. 15, 16). So again, 'the soul that hath touched any such' uncleanness 'shall be unclean until even, and shall not eat of the holy things,' much less come within the inner veil, 'unless he wash his flesh with water' (Lev. 22. 4–6). Now I would ask, what all this should signify, if a sinner, as a sinner, before he washes, or is washed, may immediately go unto the throne of grace? Yea, I ask again, why the apostle supposes washing as a preparation to the Hebrews entering into the Holiest, if men

[103]

may go immediately from under convictions to a throne of grace? For thus, he says, 'let us draw near (to "the holiest,") with a true heart, in full assurance of faith; having our hearts sprinkled from an evil conscience, and our bodies washed with pure water' (Heb. 10. 19, 22). Let us draw near; he says not that we may have; but having *first* been washed and sprinkled.

The laver then must first be washed in; and he that washed not first there, has not the right to come to the throne of grace. Wherefore you have here also a sea of glass standing before the throne of grace, to signify this thing (Rev. 4. 6). It stands before the throne for them to wash in that would indeed approach the throne of grace. For this sea of glass is the same that is shadowed forth by the laver made mention of before, and by the brazen sea that stood in Solomon's temple, whereat they were to wash before they went into the Holiest. But you may ask me, What the laver or molten sea should signify to us in the New Testament? I answer, It signifies the word of the New Testament, which contains the cleansing doctrine of remission of sins, by the precious blood of Jesus Christ (John 15. 3). Wherefore we are said to be clean through the Word, through the washing of water by the Word (Titus 3. 5). The meaning then is, A man must first come to Christ, as set forth in the Word, which is this sea of glass, before he can come to Christ in Heaven, as he is the throne of grace. For the Word, I say, is this sea of glass that stands before the throne, for the sinner to wash in first. Know therefore, whoever you are that is minded to be saved, you must begin with Christ crucified, and with the promise of remission of sins through his blood; which crucified Christ you will not find in Heaven as such; for there he is alive; but you will find him in the Word; for there he is to this day set forth in all the circumstances of his death, as crucified before our eyes (Gal. 3. 1, 2). There you will find that he died, when he died, what death he died, why he died, and the Word open to you to come and wash in his blood. The word therefore of Christ's Testament is the laver for all New Testament priests—and every Christian is a priest to God—to wash in.

Here therefore you must receive your justification, and that before you go one step further; for if you are not justified by his blood, you will not be saved by his life. And the justifying efficacy of his blood is left behind, and is here contained in the molten sea, or laver, or word of grace, for you to wash in. Indeed, there is an interceding voice in his blood for us before the throne of grace, or mercy-seat; but that is still to bring us to wash, or for them that have washed therein, as it was shed upon the cross. We have boldness therefore to enter into the holiest by the blood of Jesus, that is, by faith in his blood, as shed without the gate; for as his blood was shed without the gate, so it sanctifies the believer; and makes him capable to approach the Holy of holies. Wherefore 'Jesus also, that he might sanctify the people with his own blood, suffered without the gate.' Let us by him therefore (that is, because we are first sanctified by faith in his blood) offer to God the sacrifice of praise continually, that is, the fruit of our lips, giving thanks to his name (Heb. 13. 11–15). Wherefore the laver of regeneration, or Christ set forth by the Word as crucified, is for all coming sinners to wash in unto justification; and the throne of grace is to be approached by saints, or as sinners justified by faith in a crucified Christ; and so, as washed from sin in the sea of his blood, to come to the mercy-seat.

And it is yet far more evident; for those that approach this throne of grace must do it through believing. As says the apostle, 'How shall they call on him in whom they have not believed?' (of whom they have not heard, and in whom they have not believed), for to that purpose runs the text: 'How then shall they call on him in whom they have not believed,' antecedent to their calling on him, 'and how shall they believe in him of whom they have not heard' first? (Rom. 10. 14.) So then hearing goes before believing, and believing before calling upon God, as he sits on the throne of grace. Now, believing is to be according to the sound of the beginning of the gospel, which presents us, not first with Christ as ascended, but as dying, buried, and risen. 'For I delivered unto you first of all, that which I also received; how that Christ died for our sins according to the Scriptures; and that he was buried, and that he rose again the third day, according to the Scriptures' (1 Cor. 15. 3, 4).

I conclude then, as to this, that the order of Heaven is, that men wash in the laver of regeneration, to wit, in the blood of Christ, as held forth in the word of the truth of the gospel, which is the ordinance of God; for there sinners, as sinners, or men as unclean, may wash, in order to their approach to God as he sits upon the throne of grace.

And besides, Is it possible that a man that passes by the doctrine of Christ as dead, should be admitted with acceptance to a just and holy God for life; or that he that slights and tramples under foot the blood of Christ, as shed upon the cross, should be admitted to an interest in Christ, as he is the throne of grace? It cannot be. He must then wash there first, or die—let his profession, or pretended faith, or holiness, be what it will. For God sees iniquity in all men; nor can all the nitre or soap in the world cause that our iniquity should not be marked before God (Jer. 2. 22). 'For without shedding of blood is no remission' (Heb. 9. 22). Nothing that pollutes, that defiles, or that is unclean, must enter into God's sanctuary, much less into the most holy part thereof; but by their sacrifice, by which they are purged, and for the sake of the perfection thereof, they believing are accepted. We have 'therefore, brethren, boldness to enter into the Holiest by the blood of Jesus,' and no way else (Heb. 10. 19).

But this will yet be further manifest by what we have yet to say of the manner of our approach unto the throne of grace.

4

HOW WE ARE TO APPROACH THE
THRONE OF GRACE

━━━━━

We are to approach the throne of grace thus:

1. We must approach the throne of grace *by the second veil*; for the throne of grace is after the second veil. So, then, though a man went into the tabernacle or temple, which was a figure of the church, yet if he entered but within the first veil, he only came where there was no mercy-seat or throne of grace (Heb. 9. 3). And what is this second veil, in, at, or through which, as the phrase is, we must, by blood, enter into the Holiest? Why, as to the law, the second veil did hang up between the holy and the most holy place, and it did hide what was within the Holiest from the eyes or sight of those that went no further than into the first tabernacle. Now this second veil in the tabernacle or temple was a figure of the second veil that all those must go through that will approach the throne of grace; and that veil is the flesh of Christ.

This is that which the holy apostle testifies in his exhortation, where he says, We have 'boldness to enter into the Holiest by the blood of Jesus, by a new and living way which he hath consecrated for us through the veil, that is to say, his flesh' (Heb. 10. 19, 20). The second veil then is the flesh of Christ, the which until a man can enter or go through by his faith, it is impossible that he should come to the Holiest where the throne of grace is, that is, to the heart and soul of Jesus, which is the throne. The body of Christ is the tabernacle of God, and so that

[107]

in which God dwells; for the fulness of the Godhead dwells in him bodily (Col 2. 9). Therefore, as also has been hinted before, Christ Jesus is the throne of grace. Now, since his flesh is called the veil, it is evident that the glory that dwells within him, namely, God resting in him, cannot be understood but by them that by faith can look through, or enter through, his flesh to that glory. For the glory is within the veil; there is the mercy-seat, or throne of grace; there sits God as delighted, as at rest, in and with sinners that come to him by and through that flesh, and the offering of it for sin without the gate. 'I am the way,' says Christ; but to what? and how? (John 14. 6). Why, to the Father, through my flesh. 'And having made peace through the blood of his cross, by him to reconcile all things to himself; by him, I say, whether they be things in earth, or things in heaven. And you that were sometime alienated, and enemies in your mind by wicked works, yet now hath he reconciled (but how?) in the body of his flesh, (that then must be first: to what end?) to present you holy and unblameable, and unreprovable in his sight' (Col. 1. 20–22). That is, when you enter into his presence, or approach by this flesh, the mercy-seat, or the throne of grace.

This therefore is the manner of our coming, if we come aright to the throne of grace for mercy; we must come by blood through his flesh, as through the veil; by which, until you have entered through it, the glory of God, and His will that grace shall reign, will be utterly hid from your eyes. I will not say, but by the notion of these things, men may have their whirling fancies, and may create to themselves wild notions and flattering imaginations of Christ, the throne of grace, and of glory; but the gospel knowledge of this is of absolute necessity to my right coming to the throne of grace for mercy. I must come by his blood, through his flesh, or I cannot come at all, for there is no back door. This then is the sum, Christ's body is the tabernacle, the Holiest. 'Thy law,' says he, 'is within my heart,' or as it is the margin 'in the midst of my bowels' (Ps. 40. 7, 8). In this tabernacle then God sits, namely, on the heart of Christ, for that is the throne of grace. Through this tabernacle men must

enter, that is, by a godly understanding of what by this tabernacle or flesh of Christ has been done to reconcile us to God
that dwells in him. This is the way, all the way, for there is no
way but this to come to the throne of grace. This is the new
way into the heavenly paradise, for the old way is hedged and
ditched up by the flaming sword of cherubims (Gen. 3. 24). It
is the *new* and *living* way, for to go the other is present death.
So then, this 'new and living way which he hath consecrated
for us through the veil, that is to say, his flesh,' is the only way
into the Holiest, where the throne of grace is (Heb. 10. 20).

2. We must approach this throne of grace, *as having our
hearts, first, sprinkled from an evil conscience*. The priest that
represented all Israel, when he went into the Holiest, was not
to go in, but as sprinkled with blood first (Exod. 29. 20–21).
Thus it is written in the law; 'not without blood'; and thus it is
written in the gospel (Heb. 9. 7). And now since by the gospel
we all have admittance to enter in through the veil, by faith,
we must take heed that we enter not in without blood; for if
the blood, virtually, be not seen upon us, we die, instead of
obtaining mercy, and finding the help of grace. This I press
the oftener, because there is nothing to which we are more
naturally inclined, than to forget this. Who, that understands
himself, is not sensible how apt he is to forget to act faith in the
blood of Jesus, and to get his conscience sprinkled with the
virtue of that, as he attempts to approach the throne of grace?
Yet the Scripture calls upon us to take heed that we neglect
not thus to prepare ourselves. 'Let us draw near with a true
heart, in full assurance of faith, having our hearts sprinkled
from an evil conscience,' namely, with the blood of Christ, lest
we die (Heb. 10. 22; 9. 14). In the law all the people were to be
sprinkled with blood, and it was necessary that the patterns of
things in the heavens should be purified with these, that is, with
the blood of bulls but the heavenly things themselves with
better sacrifices than these, that is, with the offering of the
body, and shedding of the blood of Christ. By this then must

you be purified and sprinkled, who by Christ would approach the throne of grace.

3. Therefore it is added, '*And our bodies washed with pure water*.' This the apostle takes also out of the law, where it was appointed, as was showed before. Christ also, just before he went to the Father, gave his disciples a signification of this, saying to Peter, and by him to all the rest, 'If I wash thee not, thou hast no part with me' (John 13. 8). This pure water is nothing but the wholesome doctrine of the Word mixed with the Spirit, by which, as the conscience was before sprinkled with blood, the body and outward conversation is now sanctified and made clean. 'Now ye are clean through the word,' says Christ, 'which I have spoken unto you' (John 15. 3). Hence, washing, and sanctifying, and justifying, are put together, and are said to come in the name of our Lord Jesus Christ, and by the Spirit of our God (1 Cor. 6. 11). You must then be washed with water, and sprinkled with blood, if you would orderly approach the throne of grace : if you would orderly approach it with a true heart, in full assurance of faith; or if you would do as the text bids you here, namely, 'come boldly unto the throne of grace, to obtain mercy, and find grace to help in time of need.'

To tell you what it is to come boldly, is one thing; and to tell you how you should come boldly, is another. Here you are bid to come boldly, and are also showed how that may be done. It may be done through the blood of sprinkling, and through the sanctifying operations of the Spirit which are here by faith to be received. And when what can be said shall be said to the utmost, there is no boldness, godly boldness, but by blood. The more the conscience is a stranger to the sprinkling of blood, the further off it is from being rightly bold with God, at the throne of grace; for it is the blood that makes the atonement, and that gives boldness to the soul (Lev. 17. 11; Heb. 10. 19). It is the blood, the power of it by faith upon the conscience, that drives away guilt, and so fear, and consequently that begets boldness. Wherefore, he that will be bold with God at the throne of grace must first be well acquainted with the doctrine of the blood of Christ; namely, that it was shed, and why, and that it has made peace with God, and for whom. Yea, you must be able by faith to bring thyself within the number of those that are made partakers of this reconciliation, before you can come boldly to the throne of grace.

What it is to come to the throne of grace without boldness

1. There is a coming to the throne of grace before or without this boldness; but that is not the coming to which by these texts we are exhorted. Yet that coming, be it never so deficient, if it is right, is in some measure an inlet into the death and blood of Christ, and a means, though perhaps scarce at all discerned of the soul, to hope for grace from the throne. I say, the encouragement must arise from the cross, and from Christ as dying there. Christ himself went that way to God, and it is not possible but we must go the same way too. So, then, the encouragement, be it little, be it much—and it is little or much, even as the faith which apprehends Christ is little or much—is according to the proportion of faith; strong faith gives great boldness, weak faith does not so, nor can it.

2. There is a sincere coming to the throne of grace without this boldness, even a coming in the uprightness of one's heart without it. Hence a true heart and full assurance are distinguished. 'Let us draw near with a true heart, in full assurance of faith' (Heb. 10. 22). Sincerity may be attended with a great deal of weakness, even as boldness may be attended with pride; but be it what kind of coming to the throne of grace it will, either a coming with boldness, or with that doubting which is incident to saints, still the cause of that coming, or ground thereof, is some knowledge of redemption by blood, redemption which the soul sees it has faith in, or would see it has faith in. For Christ is precious, sometimes in the sight of his worth, sometimes in the sight of the want of him, and sometimes in the sight of the enjoyment of him.

3. There is an earnest coming to the throne of grace even with all the desire of one's soul. When David had guilt and

trouble, and that so heavy that he knew not what to do, yet he could say, 'Lord, all my desire is before thee, and my groaning is not hid from thee' (Ps. 38. 1–9). He could come earnestly to the throne of grace; he could come thither with all the desire of his soul; but still this must be from the knowledge that he had of the way of remission of sins by the blood of the Son of God.

4. There is also a constant coming to the throne of grace. 'Lord,' said Heman, 'I have cried day and night before thee: let my prayer come before thee: incline thine ear unto my cry, for my soul is full of troubles: and my life draweth nigh unto the grave' (Ps. 88. 1–3). Here you see is constant crying before the throne of grace, crying night and day; and yet the man that cries seems to be in a very black cloud, and to find hard work to bear up in his soul. Yet this he had, namely, the knowledge of how God was the God of salvation; yea, he called him his God as such, though with pretty much difficulty of spirit, to be sure. Wherefore it must not be concluded, that they come not at all to the throne of grace, that come not with a full assurance; or that men must forbear to come, till they come with assurance. But this I say, they come not at all aright, that take not the ground of their coming from the death and blood of Christ; and that they that come to the throne of grace, with but little knowledge of redemption by blood, will come with but little hope of obtaining grace and mercy to help in time of need.

I conclude then, that it is the privilege, the duty and glory of a man, to approach the throne of grace as a prince, as Job said, could he but find it, he would be sure to do. 'O that I knew where I might find him!' says he, 'that I might come even to his seat: I would order my cause before him, and fill my mouth with arguments: I would know the words which he would answer me, and understand what he would say unto me. Will he plead against me with his great power? No; but he would put strength in me. There the righteous might dispute with him: so should I be delivered for ever from my judge' (Job 23. 3–7). Indeed, God sometimes tries us. 'He holdeth back,' sometimes, 'the face of his throne, and spreadeth his cloud upon it' (Job 26. 9). And this seems to be Job's case here, which made him to confess he was at a loss, and to cry out, 'O that I knew where I might find him!' And this God does for trial, and to prove our honesty and constancy; for the hypocrite will not pray always. Will he always call upon God? No, verily; especially not when God binds him, afflicts him, and praying becomes hard work to him (Job 36. 13).

But difficulty as to finding of God's presence, and the sweet shining of the face of his throne, does not always lie in the weakness of faith. Strong faith may be in this perplexity, and may be hard put to it to stand at times. It is said here, that God did hold back the face of his throne, and did spread a cloud upon it; not to weaken Job's faith, but to try Job's strength, and to show to men of after ages how valiant a man Job was. Faith, if it be strong, will play the man in the dark; will, like a mettled horse, flounce [1] in a difficult way, will not be discouraged at trials, at many or strong trials: 'Though he slay me, yet will I trust in him,' is the language of that invincible grace of God (Job 13. 15). There is also an aptness in those that come to the throne of grace, to suppose that all faith is alike, whether weak or strong, and that, if it is indeed true faith, it will do so and so, even those things that the highest degrees of faith will do. Alas! faith is sometimes in a calm, sometimes up, and sometimes down, and sometimes at it with sin, death, and the devil; as we say, in blood up to the ears. Faith now has but little time to speak peace to the conscience; it is now struggling for life, it is now fighting with angels, with infernals; all it can do now, is to cry, groan, sweat, fear, fight, and gasp for life.

Indeed the soul should now run to the cross, for there is the water, or rather the blood and water, that is provided for faith, as to the maintaining of the comfort of justification; but the soul whose faith is thus attacked will find it hard work to do this, though much of the well-managing of faith, in the good fight of faith, will lie in the soul's hearty and constant adhering

[1] Flounce = rear and plunge violently.

to the death and blood of Christ; but a man must do as he can. Thus now have I showed you the manner of right coming to the throne of grace, for mercy and grace to help in time of need.

None but the godly know the throne of grace

It is the privilege of the godly to distinguish from all thrones whatsoever this throne of grace. This, as I told you before, I gathered from the apostle in the text, for he only makes mention thereof, but gives no sign to distinguish it by; no sign, I say, though he knew that there were more thrones than it. 'Let us come boldly,' says he, 'to the throne of grace,' and so leaves it, knowing full well that they had a good understanding of his meaning, being Hebrews (Heb. 9. 1–8). They were also enlightened from what they were taught by the placing of the ark of the testimony and the mercy-seat in the most holy place; of which particular the apostle did then count it not of absolute necessity distinctly to discourse. Indeed the Gentiles, as I have showed, have this throne of grace described and set forth before them, by those tokens which I have touched upon in the pages that go before. With the book of Revelation the Gentiles are particularly concerned, for it was writ to churches of the Gentiles; also the great things prophesied of there relate unto Gentile believers, and to the downfall of Antichrist, as he stands among them.

But yet, I think that John's discourse of the things attending the throne of grace were not by him so much propounded because the Gentiles were incapable of finding of it without such description, as to show the answerableness of the antitype with the type; and also to strengthen their faith, and illustrate the thing; for they that know, may know more, and better of what they know; yea, may be greatly comforted with another's dilating on what they know. Besides, the Holy Ghost by the Word doth always give the most perfect description of things; wherefore to that we should have recourse for the completing of our knowledge. I mean not, by what I say, in the least to intimate, as if this throne of grace was to be known without the

Word, for it is that that giveth revelation of Jesus Christ: but my meaning is, that a saint, as such, has such a working of things upon his heart, as makes him able by the Word to find out this throne of grace, and to distinguish it to himself from others.

1. The saint has strong guilt of sin upon his conscience, especially at first; and this makes him better judge what grace, in its nature, is, than others can that are not sensible of what guilt is. What it was to be saved, was better relished by the jailor when he was afraid of and trembled at the apprehensions of the wrath of God, than ever it was with him all his life before (Acts 16. 29-33). Peter then also saw what saving was, when he began to sink into the sea: 'Lord, save me,' said he, I perish (Matt. 14. 30). Sin is that without a sense of which a man is not apprehensive what grace is. Sin and grace, favour and wrath, death and life, hell and heaven, are opposites, and are set off, or out, in their evil or good, shame or glory, one by another. What makes grace so good to us as sin in its guilt and filth? What makes sin so horrible and damnable a thing in our eyes, as when we see there is nothing can save us from it but the infinite grace of God? Further, there seems, if I may so term it, to be a kind of natural instinct in the new creature to seek after the grace of God; for so says the Word, 'They that are after the flesh, do mind the things of the flesh; but they that are after the Spirit, the things of the Spirit' (Rom. 8. 5). The child by nature nuzzles in its mother's bosom for the breast; the child by grace does by grace seek to live by the grace of God. All creatures, the calf, the lamb, and others, so soon as they are fallen from their mother's belly, will by nature look for, and turn themselves towards the teat, and the new creature doth so too (1 Pet. 2. 1-3). For guilt makes it hunger and thirst, as the hunted hart pants after the water brooks. Hunger directs to bread, thirst directs to water; yea, it calls bread and water to mind. Let a man be doing other business, hunger will put him in mind of his cupboard, and thirst of his cruse of water; yea, it will call him, make him, force him, command him, to bethink what nourishing victuals is, and will also drive him to

search out after where he may find it, to the satisfying of himself. All right talk also to such an one sets the stomach and appetite a craving; yea, into a kind of running out of the body after this bread and water, that it might be fed, nourished, and filled therewith. Thus it is by nature, and thus it is by grace; thus it is for the bread that perishes, and for that which endures to everlasting life.

2. As nature, the new nature, teaches this by a kind of heavenly natural instinct; so experience also herein helps the godly much. For they have found all other places, the throne of grace excepted, empty, and places or things that hold no water. They have been to Mount Sinai for help, but could find nothing there but fire and darkness, but thunder and lightning, but earthquake and trembling, and a voice of killing words, which words they that heard them once could never endure to hear them again; and as for the sight of vengeance there revealed against sin, it was so terrible, that Moses, even Moses, said, 'I exceedingly fear and quake' (Heb. 12. 18–21; Exod. 19; 2 Cor. 3). They have sought for grace by their own performance; but alas! they have yielded them nothing but wind and confusion; not a performance, not a duty, not an act in any part of religious worship, but they looking upon it in the glass of the Lord, do find it spaked [1] and defective (Is. 64. 5–8). They have sought for grace by their resolutions, their vows, their purposes, and the like; but alas; they all do as the other, discover that they have been very imperfectly managed, and so such as can by no means help them to grace. They have gone to their tears, their sorrow, and repentance, if perhaps they might have found some help there; but all has either fled away like the early dew, or if they have stood, they have stunk even in the nostrils of those whose they were. How much more, then, in the nostrils of a holy God!

They have gone to God, as the great Creator, and have beheld how wonderful his works have been. They have looked to the heavens above, to the earth beneath, and to all their ornaments, but neither have these, nor what is of them, yielded grace to

---

[1] Spaked = spotted.

those that had sensible want thereof. Thus have they gone, as I said, with these pitchers to their fountains, and have returned empty and ashamed. They found no water, no river of water of life. They have been as the woman with her bloody issue, spending and spending till they have spent all, and been nothing better, but rather grew worse (Mark 5. 26). Had they searched into nothing but the law, it had been sufficient to convince them that there was no grace, nor throne of grace, in the world. For since the law, being the most excellent of all the things of the earth, is found to be such as yields no grace—for grace and truth comes by Jesus Christ, not by Moses (John 1. 17) —how can it be imagined that it should be found in anything inferior? Paul, therefore, not finding it in the law, despairs to find it in anything else below, but presently betakes himself to look for it there where he had not yet sought it—for he sometime sought it not by faith, but as it were by the works of the law (Phil. 3. 6–8)—he looked for it, I say, by Jesus Christ, who is the throne of grace, where he found it, and rejoiced in hope of the glory of God (Rom. 9. 29–31; 5. 1–3).

3. Saints come to know and distinguish the throne of grace from other thrones, by the very direction of God himself. As it is said of the well that the nobles digged in the wilderness— they digged it by the direction of the lawgiver—so saints find out the throne of grace by the direction of the grace-giver. Hence Paul prays, that the Lord would direct the hearts of the people into the love of God (2 Thess. 3. 5). Man, as man, cannot aim directly at this throne; but will drop his prayers short, besides, or the like, if he be not helped by the Spirit (Rom. 8. 26). Hence the Son says of himself, 'No man can come to me, except the Father which hath sent me draw him' (John 6. 44). Which text not only justifies what is now said, but insinuates that there is an unwillingness in man of himself to come to this throne of grace; he must be drawn thereto. God sets us in the way of his steps, that is, in that way to the throne by which grace and mercy is conveyed unto us.

4. We know the throne of grace from other thrones, by the glory that it always appears in, when revealed to us of God. Its

5

MOTIVES FOR COMING BOLDLY TO
THE THRONE OF GRACE

———

I come now to the motives by which the apostle stirs up the
Hebrews, and encourages them to come boldly to the throne of
grace. The first is, because we have there such an high priest, or
an high priest so and so qualified. Second, because we that come
thither for grace are sure there to speed, or find grace and obtain
it.

BECAUSE WE HAVE SUCH AN HIGH PRIEST THERE

As for the first of these motives, we have an encouragement
to move us to come with boldness to the throne of grace, because we have an high priest there; because we have such an
high priest there. 'For we have not an high priest which cannot
be touched with the feeling of our infirmities, but was in all
points tempted like as we are, yet without sin. Let us therefore come boldly unto the throne of grace.' Of this high priest
I have already made mention before, so far as to show you that
Christ Jesus is he, as also that he is the altar, and sacrifice, and
throne of grace, before which he also himself makes intercession. But forasmuch as by the apostle here, he is not only
presented unto us as a throne of grace, but as an high priest
ministering before it, it will not be amiss if I do somewhat
particularly treat of his priesthood also. But the main or chief
aim of my discourse will be to treat of his qualifications for his
office, which I find to be in general of two sorts: (1) Legal.
(2) Natural.

The legal qualifications of Jesus Christ for the office of high priest

When I say legal, I mean, as the apostle's expression is, not by 'the law of a carnal commandment,' but by an eternal coven-ant, and 'the power of an endless life' thereby: of which the priesthood of old was but a type, and the law of their priesthood but a shadow (Heb. 7. 16; 9. 15, 24). But because their law, and their entrance into their priesthood thereby, was, as I said, 'a shadow of good things to come,' therefore where it will help to illustrate, we will make use thereof so to do; and where not, there will we let it pass (Heb. 10. 1). The thing to be now spoken to is, that the consideration of Jesus Christ being an high priest before the throne of grace, is a motive and encouragement to us to come boldly thither for grace: 'Seeing then that we have a great high priest that is passed into the heavens, Jesus the Son of God, let us hold fast our profession,' and 'come boldly unto the throne of grace' (Heb. 4. 14, 16). Now, how was he made an high priest? for so is the expression, 'made a high priest for ever after the order of Melchisedec' (Heb. 6. 20).

First. He took not this honour upon himself without a lawful call thereto. Thus the priests under the law were put into office; and thus it was with the Son of God. 'No man taketh this honour to himself, but he that is called of God, as was Aaron. So also Christ glorified not himself to be made an high priest, but he that said unto him, Thou art my Son, to-day have I begotten thee.' Wherefore he was 'called of God an high priest after the order of Melchisedec' (Heb. 5. 4-6, 10). Thus far, therefore, the law of his priesthood answers to the law of the priesthood of old; they both were made priests by a legal call to their work or office. But yet the law by which this Son was made high priest excels, and that in these particulars—

1. He was made a priest after the similitude of Melchisedec, for he testifies, 'Thou art a priest for ever after the order of Melchisedec' (Heb. 7. 17). But they under the law were not

made priests but after the order of Aaron, that is, by a carnal commandment, not by an everlasting covenant of God.

2. And, says he, 'Inasmuch as not without an oath he was made priest, for those priests were made without an oath, but this with an oath, by him that said unto him, The Lord sware, and will not repent, Thou are a priest for ever after the order of Melchisedec' (Heb. 7. 20, 21).

3. The priesthood under the law, with their law and sacrifices, were fading, and were not suffered to continue, by reason of the death of the priest. and ineffectualness of his offering (Heb. 7. 23). 'But this man, because he continueth ever, hath an unchangeable priesthood' (ver. 24). 'For the law maketh men high priests which have infirmity, but the word of the oath which was since the law, maketh the Son, who is consecrated for evermore' (ver. 28). From what has already been said, we gather:

(1) What manner of person he is. He is the Son, the Son of God, Jesus the Son of God. Hence the apostle says, 'We have a great high priest,' such an high priest 'that is passed into the heavens' (Heb. 4. 14). Such an high priest as is 'made higher than the heavens' (Heb. 7. 26). And why does he thus dilate upon the dignity of his person, but because thereby is insinuated the excellency of his sacrifice, and the prevalency of his intercession, by that, to God for us. Therefore he says again, 'Every' Aaronical 'priest standeth daily ministering and offering oftentimes the same sacrifices, which can never take away sins; but this man,' this great man, this Jesus, this Son of God, 'after he had offered one,' one only, one once, but one (Heb. 9. 25, 26) 'sacrifice for sins for ever, sat down on the right hand of God; from henceforth expecting till his enemies be made his footstool. For by one offering he hath perfected for ever them that are sanctified' (Heb. 10. 11–14). Thus, I say, the apostle touches upon the greatness of his person, thereby to set forth the excellency of his sacrifice, and the prevalency of his intercession. 'Wherefore, holy brethren, partakers of the heavenly calling, consider the Apostle and High Priest of our profession,

Christ Jesus' (Heb. 3. 1). Or, as he says again, making mention of Melchisedec, 'Consider how great this man was (Heb. 7. 4). We have such a high priest, so great a high priest; one that is entered into the heavens: Jesus the Son of God.

(2) The manner also of his being called to and stated [1] in his office, is not to be overlooked. He is made a priest after the power of an endless life, or is to be such an one as long as he lives, and as long as we have need of his mediation. Now Christ being raised from the dead, dies no more; death has no more dominion over him. He is himself the Prince of life. Wherefore it follows, 'he hath an unchangeable priesthood.' And what then? Why, then 'he is able also to save them to the uttermost that come unto God by him, seeing he ever liveth to make intercession for them' (Heb. 7. 24, 25). But again, he is made a priest with an oath. 'The Lord sware, and will not repent, Thou art a priest for ever.' Hence I gather, (a) That before God there is no high priest but Jesus, nor ever shall be. (b) That God is to the full pleased with his high priesthood; and so with all those for whom he makes intercession. For this priest, though he is not accepted for the sake of another, yet he is upon the account of another. 'For every high priest taken from among men is ordained for men in things pertaining to God,' to make reconciliation for the sins of the people (Heb. 5. 1, 2). And again, he is entered 'into heaven itself, now to appear in the presence of God for us' (Heb. 9. 24). God therefore, in that he has made him a priest with an oath, and also determined that he will never repent of his so doing, declares that he is, and for ever will be, satisfied with his offering. And this is a great encouragement to those that come to God by him; they have by this oath a firm ground to go upon. And the oath is, 'Thou art a priest for ever': thou shalt be accepted for ever for every one for whom thou makest intercession; nor will I ever reject any body that comes to me by thee. Therefore here is ground for faith, for hope and rejoicing; for this consideration a man has ground to come boldly to the throne of grace.

[1] Instituted, installed.

Secondly. But again, as Christ is made a priest by call and with an oath, and so far, legally; so he, being thus called, has other preparatory legal qualifications. The high priest under the law was not by law to come into the Holiest, but in those robes that were ordained for him to minister in before God; which robes were not to be made according to the fancy of the people, but according to the commandment of Moses (Exod. 28). Christ our high priest in heaven has also his holy garment, with which he covers the nakedness of them that are his, which robe was not made of corruptible things, as silver and gold, but by a patient continuance in a holy life, according to the law of Moses, both moral and ceremonial. Not that either of these was that eternal testament by which he was made a priest; but the moral law was to be satisfied, and the types of the ceremonial law to be as to this eminently fulfilled; and he was bound to do so by that eternal covenant by which he is made a mediator. Wherefore, before he could enter the Holiest of all, he must have these holy garments made; neither did he trust others, as in the case of Aaron, to make these garments for him, but he wrought them all himself, according to all that Moses commanded.

Christ was a great while a-making this garment. What time, you may ask, was required? And I answer, All the days of his life; for all things that were written concerning him, as to this, were not completed till the day that he hung upon the cross. For then it was that he said, 'It is finished; and he bowed his head, and gave up the ghost' (John 19. 28–30). This robe is for glory and for beauty. This is it that (as afore I said) was of the colour of the rainbow, and that compasses even round about this throne of grace, unto which we are bid to come. This is that garment that reaches down to his feet, and that is girt to him with a golden girdle (Rev. 1. 13). This is that garment that covers all his body mystical, and that hides the blemishes of such members from the eye of God, and of the law. And it is made up of his obedience to the law, by his complete perfect obedience thereto (Rom. 5. 19). This Christ wears always, he never puts it off, as the Aaronic high priests put off theirs by a ceremonial command. He ever lives to make intercession; consequently he ever wears this priestly robe. He might not go into the holy place without it, upon danger of death, or at least of being sent back again; but he died not, but lives ever; is not sent back, but is set down at God's right hand; and there shall sit till his foes are made his footstool (John 16. 10).

This is that for the sake of which all are made welcome, and embraced and kissed, forgiven and saved, that come unto God by him. This is that righteousness, that mantle spotless, that Paul so much desired to be found wrapt in; for he knew that being found in that he must be presented thereby to God a glorious man, not having spot, or wrinkle, or any such thing. This therefore is another of the Lord Jesus's legal qualifications, as preparatory to the executing of his high priest's office in heaven. But of this something has been spoken before; and therefore I shall not enlarge upon it here.

Thirdly. When the high priest under the law was thus instituted by a legal call, and a garment suitable to his office, then again there was another thing that must be done, in order to his regular execution of his office; and that was, he must be consecrated, and solemnly ushered thereunto by certain offerings, first presented to God for himself. This you have mention made of in the Levitical law; you have there first commanded, that, in order to the high priest's approaching the Holiest for the people, there must first be an offering of consecration for himself, and this is to follow his call, and the finishing of his holy garments (Exod. 25. 5–7, 19–22). For this ceremony was not to be observed until his garments were made and put upon him; also the blood of the ram of consecration was to be sprinkled upon him and his garments, that he might be hallowed, and rightly set apart for the high priest's office (Lev. 8). The Holy Ghost, I think, thus signifying that Jesus the Son of God, our great high priest, was not only to sanctify the people with his blood, but first, by blood must to that work be sanctified himself; 'For their sakes,' says he, 'I sanctify myself, that they also might be sanctified through the truth' (John 17. 19).

But it may be asked, When was this done to Christ, or what sacrifice of consecration had he earlier than the offering up of himself for our sins? I answer, It was done in the garden when he was washed in his own blood, when his sweat was as great drops of blood, falling down to the ground. For there it was he was sprinkled with his blood, not only the tip of his ear, his thumb, and toe, but there he was washed all over; there therefore was his most solemn consecration to his office; at least, so I think. And this, as Aaron's was, was done by Moses; it was Moses that sprinkled Aaron's garments. It was by virtue of an agony also that Christ's bloody sweat was produced; and what was the cause of that agony, but the apprehension of the justice and curse of Moses's law, which now he was to undergo for the sins of the people.

With his sacrifice he then subjoined another, which was also preparatory to the great acts of his high priest's office, which he was afterwards to perform for us. And that was his drink-offering, his tears, which were offered to God with strong cries (Exod. 29. 40; Num. 28. 7). For this was the place and time that in a special manner he caused his strong wine to be poured out, and that he drank his tears as water. This is called his offering, his offering for his own acceptance with God. After 'he had offered up prayers and supplications, with strong crying and tears unto him that was able to save him,' he 'was heard' for his piety, for his acceptance as to this office, for he merited his office as well as his people (Heb. 5. 7). Wherefore it follows, 'and being made perfect,' that is, by a complete performance of all that was necessary for the orderly attaining of his office as high priest, 'he became the author of eternal salvation unto all them that obey him' (Heb. 5. 9).

For your better understanding of me as to this, keep in mind that I speak of a twofold perfection in Christ; one as to his person, the other as to his performances. In the perfection of his person, two things are to be considered; first, the perfection of his humanity, as to the nature of it. It was at first appearing, wholly without pollution of sin, and so completely perfect; but yet this humanity was to have joined to this another perfection—a perfection of stature and age. Hence it is said that as to his humanity he increased, that is, grew more perfect. For this his increasing was in order to a perfection, not of nature, simply as nature, but of stature. 'Jesus increased in wisdom and stature' (Luke 2. 52). The paschal lamb was a lamb the first day it was yeaned; but it was not to be sacrificed until it attained such a perfection of age as by the law of God was appointed to it (Exod. 12. 5, 6). It was necessary, therefore, that Christ as to his person should be perfect in both these senses. And indeed 'in due time Christ died for the ungodly' (Rom. 5. 6).

Again, as there was a perfection of person, or of nature and personage in Christ, so there was to be a perfection of performances in him also. Hence it is said, that Jesus increased in favour with God (Luke 2. 52); that is, by the perfecting of his obedience to him for us. Now, his performances were such as had a respect to his bringing in of righteousness for us in the general; or such as respected preparations for his sacrifice as a high-priest. But let them be applied to both, or to this or that in particular. It cannot be, that while the most part of his performances were wanting, he should be as perfect as when he said, 'The things concerning me have an end' (Luke 22. 37).

Not but that every act of his obedience was perfect, and carried in it a length and breadth proportionable to that law by which it was demanded. Nor was there at any time in his obedience that which made one commandment to interfere with another. He did all things well, and so stood in the favour of God. But yet one act was not actually all, though virtually any one of his actions might carry in it a merit sufficient to satisfy and quiet the law. Hence, as I said, it is told us, not only that he is the Son of God's love, but that he increased in favour with God; that is, by a going on in doing, by a continuing to do that always that pleased the God of heaven.

A man that pays money at the day appointed, beginning first at one shilling, or one pound, and so ceaseth not until he has in current coin counted out the whole sum to the creditor, does well at the beginning; but the first shilling, or first pound, not being the full debt, cannot be counted or reckoned the whole, but a part; yet is it not an imperfect part, nor does the creditor find fault at all, because there is but so much now counted; but concludes that all is at hand, and accepts of this first, as a first-fruits: so Christ, when he came into the world, began to pay, and so continued to do, even until he had paid the whole debt, and so increased in favour with God. There was then a gradual performance of duties, as to the number of them, by our Lord when he was in the world, and consequently a time wherein it might be said that Christ had not, as to act, done all, as was appointed him to do, to do as preparatory to that great thing which he was to do for us. Wherefore, in conclusion, he is said to be made perfect, 'and being made perfect, he became the author of eternal salvation to all them that obey him' (Heb. 5. 9).

It will be objected, then, that at some time it might be said of Christ that he was imperfect in his obedience. I answer: There was a time wherein it might have been said that Christ had not done all that he was to do for us on earth. But it does not follow thereupon, that he therefore was imperfect in his obedience; for all his acts of obedience were done in their proper time, and when they should, according to the will of God. The timing of performances adds to or diminishes from the perfection of obedience, or the imperfection of it. Had these Jews killed the passover three days sooner than the time appointed, they had transgressed (Exod. 12. 6). Had the Jews done that on the fourth day to Jericho, which was to have been done on the seventh day, they had sinned (Jos. 6. 10–16). Duty is beautiful in its time, and the Son of God observed the time. 'I must,' says he, 'work the works of him that sent me, while it is day,' that is, in their seasons.

You must keep in mind that we speak all this while of that part of Christ's perfection, as to duties, which stood in the number of performances, and not in the nature or quality of acts. And I say, as to the thing in hand, Christ had duty to do, with respect to his office as high priest for us, which immediately concerned himself; such duties as gave him a legal admittance unto the execution thereof; such duties, the which, had they not orderly been done, the want of them would have made him an undue approacher of the presence of God, in that respect. Wherefore, as I said afore, by what he did thereabout, he consecrated, or sanctified himself for that work, according to the will of God, and was accepted for his piety, or in that he feared (Heb. 5. 7), and did orderly do what he should do.

Fourthly. The next thing preparatory to the execution of this office of high priest was the sacrifice itself. The sacrifice, you know, must, as to the being of it, needs precede the offering of it; it must be before it can be offered. Nor could Christ have been an high priest, had he not had a sacrifice to offer. 'For every high priest is ordained to offer gifts and sacrifices; wherefore it is of necessity that this man have somewhat also to offer' (Heb. 8. 3). And I bring in the sacrifice as the last thing preparatory, not that it was last, as to being, for it was before he could be capable of doing any of the afore-named duties, being his body, in and by which he did them, but it was the last as to fitness; it was not to be a sacrifice before the time, the time appointed of the Father; for since he had prepared it to that end, it was fit as to the time of its being offered, that that should be when God thought best also (Heb. 10. 5).

Behold then, here is the high priest with his sacrifice; and behold again, how he comes to offer it. He comes to offer his burnt-offering at the call of God; he comes to do it in his priestly garments, consecrated and sanctified in his own blood; he comes with blood and tears, or by water and blood, and offers his sacrifice, himself a sacrifice unto God for the sin of the world; and that too at a time when God began to be weary of the service and sacrifices of all the world. 'Wherefore when he cometh into the world, he saith, Sacrifice and offering thou wouldest not, but a body hast thou prepared me,' thou hast fitted me; 'in burnt-offerings and sacrifices for sin thou hast had no pleasure; then said I, Lo I come, in the volume of the book it is written of me, to do thy will, O God' (Heb. 10. 5–7).

Thus you see our high priest proceeded to the execution of his priestly office; and now we are come to his sacrifice, we will consider a little of the parts thereof, and how he offered, and pleads the same. The burnt-offering for sin had two parts, the flesh and the fat, which fat is called the fat of the inwards, of the kidneys, and the like (Lev. 3. 12–16). Answerable to this, the sacrifice of Christ had two parts, the body and the soul. The body is the flesh, and his soul as the fat, that inward part that must not by any means be kept from the fire (Is. 53. 10). For without the burning of the fat, the burnt-offering and sin-offering, both which were a figure of the sacrifice of our high priest, were counted imperfect, and so not acceptable.

And it is observable, that in these kinds of offerings, when they were to be burned, the fat and the head must be laid and be burned together; and the priest 'shall cut it into his pieces with his head and his fat; and the priest shall lay them in order on the wood that is on the fire which is upon the altar' (Lev. 1. 2). To signify, methinks, the feeling sense that this sacrifice of his body and soul should have of the curse of God due to sin, all the while that it suffered for sin. And therefore it is from this that this sacrifice has the name of burnt-offering; it is the burnt-offering for the burning, because of the burning upon the altar all night, until the morning; and the fire of the altar shall be burning in it.

The fat made the flame to increase and to ascend; wherefore God speaks affectionately of the fat, saying, The fat of mine offerings. And again, 'He shall see of the travail of his soul *and* shall be satisfied' (Is. 53. 10–12). The soul-groans, the soul-cries, the soul-conflicts that the Son of God had, together with his soul-submission to his Father's will, when he was made a sacrifice for sin, did doubtless flame bright, ascend high, and cast out a sweet savour unto the nostrils of God, whose justice was now being appeased for the sin of men.

His flesh also was part of this sacrifice, and was made to feel that judgment of God for sin that it was capable of. And it was capable of feeling much, so long as natural life, and so, bodily sense, remained. It also began to feel with the soul, by reason of the union that was betwixt them both; the soul felt, and the body bled; the soul was in an agony, and the body sweat blood; the soul wrestled with the judgment and curse of the law, and the body, to show its sense and sympathy, sent out dolorous cries, and poured out rivers of tears before God. We will not here at large speak of the lashes, of the crown of thorns, of how his face was bluft [1] with blows and blood; also how he was wounded, pierced, and what pains he felt while life lasted, as he suffered for our sins. These things are also prefigured in the old law, by the nipping or wringing of the head, the cutting of the sacrifice in pieces, and burning it in the fire (Lev. 1). Now, you must know, that as the high priest was to offer his sacrifice, so he was to bring the blood thereof to the mercy-seat or throne of grace, where now our Jesus is; he was to offer it at the door of the tabernacle, and to carry the blood within the veil; of both which I shall speak a little.

Christ a willing and an effectual sacrifice

1. He was to offer it, and how? Not grudgingly, nor as by compulsion, but of a voluntary will and cheerful mind : 'If his offering be a burnt-sacrifice of the herd, let him offer a male without blemish; he shall offer it of his own voluntary will' (Lev. 1. 3). Thus did Christ when he offered up himself. He offered a male, 'himself,' without blemish (Heb. 7. 27). He gave himself a ransom; he 'gave his life a ransom' (Matt. 20. 28). He laid down his life of himself (John 10. 18; Luke 12. 5). He longed for the day of his death, that he might die to redeem his people. Nor was he ever so joyful in all his life, that we read of, as when his sufferings grew near; then he takes the sacrament of his body and blood into his own hands, and with thanksgiving bestows it among his disciples; then he sings an hymn, then he rejoices, then he comes with a 'Lo, I come'. O

[1] Exposed to violence—blindfolded.

the heart, the great heart, that Jesus Christ had for us to do us good! He did it with all the desire of his soul.

2. He did it, not only voluntarily, and of a free will, but of love and affection to the life of his enemies. Had he done thus for the life of his friends, it had been much; but since he did it out of love to the life of his enemies, that is much more. 'Scarcely for a righteous man will one die, yet peradventure for a good man some would even dare to die; but God commendeth his love toward us, in that, while we were yet sinners, Christ died for us' (Rom. 5. 7, 8).

3. He did it without relinquishment of mind, when he was in his pangs: no discouragement disheartened him; cry and bleed he did, yea, roar, by reason of the troubles of his soul, but his mind was fixed; his Father sware and did not repent, that he should be his priest; and he vowed, and said he would not repent that he had threatened to be the plague and death of death (Hos. 13. 13, 14).

4. He did it effectually and to purpose: he stopped the mouth of the law with blood; he so pacified justice, that it now can forgive; he carried sin away from before the face of God, and set us quit in his sight; he destroyed the devil, abolished death, and brought life and immortality to light through the gospel; he wrought such a change in the world by what he has done for them that believe, that all things work together for their good, from thenceforward and for ever.

Christ the altar

I should now come to the second part of the office of this high priest, and speak to that; as also to those things that were preparatory unto his executing it; but first, I think convenient a little to treat of the altar also upon which this sacrifice was offered to God.

Some, I conceive, have thought the altar to be the cross on which the body of Christ was crucified, when he gave himself an offering for sin. But they are greatly deceived, for he also himself was the altar through which he offered himself. This is one of the treasures of wisdom which are hid in him, and of which the world and Antichrist are utterly ignorant. I touched this in one hint before, but now a little more express. The altar is always greater than the gift; and since the gift was the body and soul of Christ—for so says the text, 'He gave himself for our sins'—the altar must be something else than a sorry bit of wood, or than a cursed tree. Wherefore I will say to such, as one wiser than Solomon said to the Jews, when they superstitiated [1] the gift, in counting it more honourable than the altar, 'Ye fools, and blind, for whether is greater, the gift, or the altar that sanctifieth the gift?' (Matt. 23. 18, 19).

If the altar be greater than the gift, and yet the gift so great a thing as the very humanity of Christ, can it—I will now direct my speech to the greatest fool—can that greater thing be the cross? Is, was the cross, the wooden cross, the cursed tree, that some worship, greater than the gift, namely, than the sacrifice which Christ offered, when he gave himself for our sins! O idolatry, O blasphemy!

But what then was the altar? I answer, the divine nature of Christ, that Eternal Spirit, by and in the assistance of which he 'offered himself without spot to God'; he, through the Eternal Spirit 'offered himself' (Heb. 9. 14).

1. And it must be that, because, as was said, the altar is greater than the gift; but there is nothing but Christ's divine nature greater than his human; to be sure, a sorry bit of wood, a tree, the stock of a tree, is not.

2. It must be Christ's divine nature, because the text says plainly that 'the altar sanctifies the gift,' that is, puts worth and virtue into it; but was it the tree, or the Godhead of Christ, that put virtue and efficacy into this sacrifice that he offered to God for us? If you can but count your fingers, judge.

3. The altar was it of old that was to bear up the sacrifice until it was consumed; and with reference to the sacrifice under consideration, the tree could not bear up that; for our sacrifice being a man, consisting of soul and body, that which could bear him up in his suffering condition, must be that that could apply itself to his reasonable and sensible part for relief and

[1] Superstitiated = the esteeming of one thing above another.

succour, and that was of power to keep him even in his spirit, and in a complete submissiveness to God, in the present condition in which he was; and could the tree do this, think you? Had the tree that command and government of the soul and sense of Christ, of the reason and feeling of the Lord Jesus, as to keep him in this bitter suffering, in that evenness and spotlessness in his torment, as to cause that he should come through this great work without the least smell or tang of imperfection? No, no! it was through the Eternal Spirit that he 'offered himself without spot to God.'

Wherefore then served the cross? I answer by asking, wherefore served the wood by which the sacrifices were burned? The sacrifices were burned with wood upon the altar; the wood then was not the altar, the wood was that instrument by which the sacrifice was consumed, and the cross that by which Christ suffered his torment and affliction. The altar then was it that did bear both the wood and sacrifice, that did uphold the wood to burn, and the sacrifice to abide the burning. And with reference to the matter in hand, the tree on which Christ was hanged, and the sacrifice of his body, were both upheld by his divine power; yet the tree was no more a sacrifice, nor an altar, than was the wood upon the altar; nor was the wood, but the fire, holy, by which the sacrifice was consumed. Let the tree then be the tree, the sacrifice the sacrifice, and the altar the altar; and let men have a care how, in their worship, they make altars upon which, as they pretend, they offer the body of Christ; and let them leave off foolishly to dote upon wood, and the works of their hands: the altar is greater than the gift or sacrifice that was, or is, upon it.

How Christ executes the office of high priest

We come now to the second part of the office of this high priest and to show how he performs it. In order to which, I must, as I did with reference to the first, show you what things, as preparatory, were to precede the execution of it. We have here, as you see, 'our passover sacrificed for us,' for our encouragement to come to the throne of grace; and now let us look to it, as it is presented in the Holiest of all, and to the order of its being so presented.

First, then, before there was anything further done—I mean by this high priest, as to a further application of his offering—the judgment of God was waited for by him, with respect to his estimation of what was already done, namely, how that was resented [1] by him; the which he declared to the full by raising him from the dead. For in that Christ was raised from the dead, when yet he died for our sins, it is evident that his offering was accepted, or esteemed of value sufficient to effect that for the which it was made a sacrifice, which was for our sins; this, therefore, was in order to his being admitted into heaven. God, by raising him from the dead, justified his death, and counted it sufficient for the saving of the world. And this Christ knew would be the effect of his death, long before he gave himself a ransom; where he says, 'This also shall please the Lord better than an ox or bullock that hath horns and hoofs' (Ps. 69. 31). And again, 'For the Lord God will help me; therefore shall I not be confounded: therefore have I set my face like a flint, and I know that I shall not be ashamed. He is near that justifieth me; who will contend with me? Let us stand together; who is mine adversary? Let him come near to me. Behold, the Lord God will help me; who is he that shall condemn me? Lo, they all shall wax old as a garment, the moth shall eat them up' (Isa. 50. 7–9). All this is the work of the Lord God, his Father, and he had faith therein, as I said before. And since it was God who was to be appeased, it was requisite that he should be heard in the matter, as to whether he was pacified or no: the which he has declared, I say, in raising him from the dead. And this the apostles, both Paul and Peter, insinuate, when they ascribe his resurrection to the power of another, rather than to his raising of himself, saying, 'This Jesus hath God raised up' (Acts 2. 32). 'God hath raised' him 'from the dead' (3. 15), 'whom God raised from the dead,' and the like (4. 10; 5. 30; 8. 56; 13. 30). I say, therefore, that God, by raising

---

[1] resented = found satisfactory.

up Christ from the dead, has said that thus far his offering pleased him, and that he was content.

But lest the world, being besotted by sin, should not rightly interpret actions, therefore God added to his raising him up from the dead, a solemn exposing of him to view, not to all men, but to such as were faithful, and that might be trusted with the communicating of it to others: 'Him,' says Peter, 'God raised' from the dead, 'and showed him openly, not to all the people, but to witnesses chosen before of God, even to us who did eat and drink with him after he rose from the dead' (Acts 10. 40, 41). And this was requisite, not because it added anything to the value and worth of his sacrifice, but for the help of the faith of them that were to have eternal salvation by him. And it is for this cause that Paul so enlarges upon this very thing, namely, that there were those that could testify that God had raised him up from the dead; so that men might see that God was well pleased, and that they had encouragement to come boldly by him to the throne of grace for mercy (1 Cor. 15. 1–8). And this exposing of him to view, was not for the length of a surprising or dazzling moment, but days and nights, to the number of no less than forty; and that to the self-same persons, namely, 'the apostles whom he had chosen: To whom also,' says the text, 'he showed himself alive after his passion, by many infallible proofs, being seen of them forty days, and speaking of the things pertaining to the kingdom of God' (Acts 1. 2, 3). Thus God therefore, being willing more abundantly to show him unto the world, ordered this great season betwixt his resurrection and ascension, that the world might see that they had ground to believe that an atonement was made for sin.

But again, a third thing that was to precede the execution of the second part of this his priestly office was, the manner and order of his going into the Holiest; I say, the manner and order of his going. He was to go thither in that robe of which mention was made before, namely, in the virtue of his obedience, for it was that which was to make his way for him as now sprinkled with his blood. He was to go thither with a noise which the Holy Ghost calls a shout, saying, 'God is gone up with a shout, the Lord with the sound of a trumpet' (Ps. 47. 5). This was prefigured by the bells, as I said, which did hang on the border of Aaron's garments. This shout seems to signify the voice of men and angels; and this trumpet the voice and joy of God; for so it says, he shall descend : 'For the Lord himself shall descend from heaven with a shout, with the voice of the arch-angel, and with the trump of God' (1 Thess. 4. 16). Even as he ascended and went up; for Aaron's bells were to be heard when he went into, and when he came out of, the holy place (Exod. 28. 33–35). But what men were to ascend with him, but, as was said afore, the men that 'came out of the graves after his resurrection?' (Matt. 27. 53). And what angels but those that ministered to him here in the day of his humiliation? As for the evil ones, he then rode in triumph over their heads, and crushed them as captives with his chariot wheels. He has ascended on high, he has 'led captivity captive, he has received gifts for men' (Eph. 4. 8).

Thus then he ascended unto and into the holy paradise, where he was waited for by a multitude of the heavenly host, and by thousands of millions of the spirits of just men made perfect. So approaching the highest heavens, the place of the special presence of God, he was bid to sit down at his right hand, in token that, for his sufferings' sake, God had made him the highest of every creature, and given him a name above every name, and commanded that now, at the name of Jesus, all things in heaven should bow, and promised, that at the day of judgment, all on earth, and under it, should bow too, to the glory of God the Father (Phil. 2. 6–11). Thus he presented himself on our behalf unto God, a sacrifice of a sweet-smelling savour, in which God rests for ever, for the blood of this sacri-fice has always with him a pleasing and prevailing voice. It cannot be denied, it cannot be outweighed by the heaviness, circumstances, or aggravations of any sin whatsoever, of them that come unto God by him. He is always in the midst of the throne, and before the throne, 'a Lamb as it had been slain, now appearing in the presence of God for us. Of the manner of his

[136]

intercession, whether it was vocal or virtual,[1] whether by voice of mouth, or merit of deed, or both, I will not determine; we know but little while here how things are done in heaven, and we may soon be too carnal, or fantastical in our apprehensions. Intercession he makes, that is, he manages the efficacy and worth of his suffering with God for us, and is always prevalent in his thus managing his merits on our behalf. And as to the manner, though it be in itself infinitely beyond what we can conceive while here, yet God has stooped to our weakness, and so expressed himself in this matter, that we might somewhat, though but childishly, apprehend him (1 Cor. 13. 11, 12). And we do not amiss if we conceive as the Word of God has revealed; for the Scriptures are the green poplar, hazel, and the chestnut rods that lie in the gutters where we should come to drink; all the difficulty lies in seeing the white strakes, the very mind of God there, that we may conceive by it.

But the text says he prays in heaven, he makes intercession there. Again, it says his blood speaks, and, consequently, why may not his groans, his tears, his sighs, and strong cries, which he uttered here in the days of flesh? I believe they do, and that they have a strong voice with God for the salvation of his people. He may then intercede both vocally and virtually; virtually to be sure he does, and we are allowed so to apprehend, because the text suggests such a manner of intercession to us. And because our weakness will not admit us to understand fully the thing as it is, our belief that he makes intercession for us has also the advantage of being purged from its faultiness by his intercession, and we shall be saved thereby, because we have relied upon his blood shed, and the prevalency of the worthiness of it with God for us; even though as to this circumstance, the manner of his interceding, we should be something at a loss.

The Word says that we have yet but the image of heavenly things, or of things in the heavens. I do not at all doubt but that many of those that were saved before Christ came in the flesh, though they were, as to the main, right, and relied upon him to

---

[1] virtual = effective in respect of inherent qualities or powers.

the saving of their souls, yet came far short of the knowledge of many of the circumstances of his suffering for them (Heb. 10. 1). Did they all know that he was to be betrayed of Judas? that he was to be scourged of the soldiers? that he was to be crowned with thorns? that he was to be crucified between two thieves, and to be pierced till blood and water came out of his side? or that he was to be buried in Joseph's sepulchre? I say, did all that were saved by faith that he was to come and die for them, understand these, with many more circumstances that were attendants of him to death? It would be rude [1] to think so; because for it we have neither Scripture nor reason. Even so, we now who believe that 'he ever liveth to make intercession for us,' are also very short of understanding of the manner or mode of his so interceding. Yet we believe that he died, and that his merits have a voice with God for us; yea, that he manages his own merits before God in a way of intercession for us, far beyond what we, while here, are able to conceive.

The Scripture says that 'all the fulness of the Godhead' dwells in him 'bodily' (Col. 2. 9). It also says that he is the throne of God, and yet again, that he sits 'on the right hand of the throne' (Is. 22. 23; Heb. 12. 2). These things are so far from being comprehended by the weakest, that they strain the wits and parts of the strongest, yet there is a heavenly truth in all. Heavenly things are not easily believed, no, not of believers themselves, while here on earth, and when they are, they are believed but weakly and infirmly. I believe that the very appearing of Christ before God is an intercession as a priest, as well as a plea of an advocate; and I believe again, that his very life there is an intercession there, a continual intercession (Heb. 9. 24; Rom. 5. 10).

But there is yet something further to be said. Christ, the humanity of Christ, if in it dwells all the fulness of the Godhead bodily, how then appears he before him to make intercession? or if Christ is the throne of grace and mercy-seat, how does he appear before God as sitting there, to sprinkle that now with his blood? Again, if Christ be the altar of incense, how

[1] rude = unlearned, inexpert.

stands he as a priest by that altar to offer the prayers of all the saints thereon, before the throne?

How these mysteries are to be learned

That all this is written is true; and that it is all truth, is as true: but that it is all understood by every one that is saved I do not believe is true. I mean, so understood as that they could all reconcile the seeming contradictions that are in these texts. There are therefore three lessons that God has set us as to the perfecting of our understanding in the mysteries of God:

1. *Letters.* I call the ceremonial law so; for there all is set forth distinctly, everything by itself, as letters are to children: there you have a priest, a sacrifice, an altar, a holy place a mercy-seat: and all distinct.

2. *Words.* Now in the gospel these letters are put all in *a word*, and Christ is that word, that word of God's mind; and therefore the gospel makes Christ that priest, Christ that sacrifice, Christ that altar, Christ that holy place, Christ that throne of grace, and all; for Christ is all. All these meet in him as several letters meet in one word.

3. *Meanings.* Next to the word you have *the meaning*, and the meaning is more difficult to be learned than either the letters or the word; and therefore the perfect understanding of that is reserved till we arrive at a higher form, till we arrive at a perfect man; 'But when that which is perfect is come, then that' knowledge 'which is in part, shall be done away' (1 Cor. 13. 10). Meantime our business is to learn to bring the letters into a word, to bring the ceremonies to Christ, and to make them terminate in him; I mean, to find the priesthood in Christ, the sacrifice in Christ, the altar in Christ, the throne of grace in Christ, and also God in Christ, reconciling the world unto himself by him. And if we can learn this well, while here, we shall not at all be blamed! For this is the utmost lesson set us, namely, to learn Christ as we find him revealed in the gospel: 'I determined,' says Paul, 'not to know any thing among you, save Jesus Christ, and him crucified (1 Cor. 2. 2). And Christians, after some time, I mean those that pray and pry into the

Word well, do attain to some good measure of knowledge of him. It is life eternal to know him, as he is to be known here, as he is to be known by the Holy Scriptures (John 17. 3). Keep then close to the Scriptures, and let your faith obey the authority of them, and you will be sure to increase in faith; 'for therein is the righteousness of God revealed from faith to faith; as it is written, The just shall live by faith' (Rom. 1. 17; 16. 25–27).

Believe then that Christ died, was buried, rose again, ascended, and ever lives to make intercession for you: and take heed of prying too far, for in mysteries men soon lose their way. It is good therefore that you rest in this, namely, that he does so, though you cannot tell how he does it. A man at court gets by his intercession a pardon for a man in the country; and the party concerned, after he has intelligence of it, knows that such an one has obtained his pardon, and that by his interceding, but for all that he may be ignorant of his methods of intercession, and so are we, at least in part, of Christ's. The meaning then is that I should believe that for Christ's sake God will save me, since he has justified me with his blood; 'being now justified by his blood, we shall be saved from wrath through him' (Rom. 5. 9). Through his intercession, or through his coming between the God whom I have offended and me, a poor sinner: through his coming between us with the voice of his blood and merits, which speaks on my behalf to God, because that blood was shed for me, and because those merits, in the benefit of them, are made over to me by an act of the grace of God, according to his eternal covenant made with Christ—this is what I know of his intercession; I mean with reference to the act itself, namely, *how* he makes intercession. And since all the fulness of the Godhead dwells in him bodily, and since he also, as to his humanity, is the throne of grace; yea, and since he also is the Holiest of all, and the rest of God for ever, it has been some scruple to me, whether it be not too carnal to imagine as if Christ stood distinct in his humanity; distinct, I say, as to space, from the Father as sitting upon a throne, and as so presenting his merits, and making vocal prayers for the life and salvation of his people. The more true meaning in my apprehension is, that the presence and worth of the human nature, being with the divine, yea, taken into union with God for ever, for the service that was done by God for it in the world, in reconciling his elect unto him, is still, and ever will be, so deserving in his sight as to prevail—I know not how else to express it—with the divine nature, in which alone is a power to subdue all impossibilities to itself, to preserve those so reconciled to eternal life.

When I speak of the human nature, I mean the man Christ, not bereft of sense and reason, nor of the power of willing and affecting [1]; but thus I mean, that the human nature so terminates in the will of the divine; and again, the will of the divine so terminates, as to saving of sinners, in the merit and will of the human, that what the Father would the Son wills, and what the Son wills the Father acquiesces in for ever. And this the Son wills, and his will is backed with infinite merit, in which also the Father rests, that those, all those whom the Father hath given him, be with him where he is, that they may behold his glory (John 17. 24). And now I am come to the will and affections of the high priest.

The natural qualifications of Jesus Christ to be our high priest

This leads me to the natural qualifications of Christ as a high priest.

First. This is one thing that I would urge, *he is not of a nature foreign to that of man.* The angels love us well, but they are not so capable of sympathising with us in our distresses, because they are not partakers of our nature. Nature has a peculiar sympathy in it; now he is naturally one with us, sin only excepted, and that is our advantage too. He is man as we are, flesh and blood as we are: born of a woman, and in all points made like unto us, that excepted which the Holy Ghost excepts. 'Forasmuch then as the children are partakers of flesh and blood, he also himself likewise took part of the same. For verily

[1] affecting = creating a disposition.

he took not on him the nature of angels, but he took on him the seed of Abraham' (Heb. 2. 14, 16). This qualifies him much; for, as I said before, there is a sympathy in nature. A man will not be so affected with the hurt that comes to a beast, as he naturally will with the hurt that comes to a man : a beast will be more affected with those attempts that are made upon its own kind to hurt it, than it will be with those that are made upon man. Wherefore? Why, there is a sympathy in nature.

Now that Christ, the high priest of the house of God, is naturally one with us, the Scriptures plainly affirm. 'God sent forth his Son, made of a woman' (Gal. 4. 4): he was 'made of the seed of David, according to the flesh' (Rom. 1. 3); from the fathers, of whom, 'as concerning the flesh Christ came' (Rom. 9. 5; 2 Tim. 2. 8). And this must needs make him a well-qualified high priest (Heb. 2. 14, 15). We will not now speak of the necessity of his taking upon him the human nature, in order that he might destroy him that had the power of death, that is, the devil, and deliver his people; for that would be here too much beside our matter, and be a diversion to the reader. We are now upon his high priest's office, and of those natural qualifications that attend him in it; and I say, nature is a great qualification, because in nature there is sympathy; and where there is sympathy, there will be a provocation to help, a provocation to help with jealousy and indignation against those that afflict. A bear robbed of her whelps is not more provoked than is the Lord Jesus when there are means used to make them miss of life eternal for whom he hath died, and for whom he ever lives to make intercession.

Secondly. As there is natural sympathy in Christ to those for whom he is an high priest, so *there is relative sympathy*. He has not only taken to or upon him our nature, but he is become one brotherhood with us. Now you know that brotherhood will carry a man further than nature; so then, when nature and relation meet, there is a double obligation. 'For both he that sanctifieth,' which is Christ, 'and they who are sanctified,' his saints, 'are all of one,' which is God; and they are all of God, as

[142]

pray before, yet they leave off to pray then. Why, these people are oftentimes ruined and undone. The reason is, this change is attended with new snares, with new cares, and with new temptations, in the which—because through unwatchfulness they are not aware—they are taken, drawn to perdition and destruction by them. Many in my short day have gone, I doubt not, down to the pit, this way, that have sometimes been to appearance the very foremost and hopefulest in the place where they have lived. O how soon has their fire gone out and their lamps ceased to burn! How quickly have they lost their love to their ministers, by whom they were illuminated, and to the warmest Christians, through communion with whom they used to be kept awake and savoury! How quickly have they found them out new friends, new companions, new ways and methods of life, and new delights to feed their foolish minds withal! Wherefore, O you that are in this matter concerned, 'Come boldly unto the throne of grace, to obtain mercy, and find grace to help in time of need.'

6. Another time of need is, when the generality of professors are decayed; when the custom of fancies and fooleries have taken away all gravity and modesty from among the children of men. Now pray, or you will die; yea, pray against those decays, those vain customs, those foolish fancies, those light and vain carriages that have overtaken others, else they will assuredly knock at your door, and obtain favour at your hand, the which if they do, they will quickly bring you down into the dirt with others, and put you in peril of damnation as well as they.

7. Another time of need is, the time of guilt contracted, and of the hiding of God's face. This is a dangerous time. If you now forbear to pray, you are undone, for the natural tendency of guilt is to drive a man from God. So it served our first father; and oft-times when God hides his face, men run into desperation, and so throw up all duties, and say as he of old, 'What should I wait for the Lord any longer?' (2 Kings 6. 33). Now your great help against this is prayer, continuing in prayer. Prayer wrestles with the devil, and will overthrow him: prayer

wrestles with God, and will overcome him: prayer wrestles with all temptations, and makes them fly. Great things have been done by prayer, even by the prayer of those that have contracted guilt, and that have by their sins lost the smiles and sense of the favour of God. Wherefore, when this needy, this evil time has overtaken you, pray: 'Come boldly unto the throne of grace, to obtain mercy, and find grace to help in time of need.'

8. The day of reproach and slander is another time of need, or a day in which you will want supplies of grace. Sometimes we meet with days wherein we are loaded with reproaches, slanders, scandals, and lies. Christ found the day of reproach a burdensome day unto him; and there is many a professor driven quite away from all conscience towards God, and open profession of his name, by such things as these (Ps. 69. 7). Reproach, when cast at a man, is as if he was being stoned to death with stones. Now ply it hard at the throne of grace, for mercy and grace to bear you up, or you will either miscarry or sink underground by the weight of reproach that may fall upon you.

9. Another time of need is that wherein a man's friends desert and forsake him, because of his gospel principles, or of those temptations that attend his profession. This is a time that often happens to those that are good. Thus it was with Christ, with Paul, with Job, with Heman, and so has it been with many other of God's servants in the day of their temptations in this world; and a sore time it is. Job complained under it, so did Heman, Paul, and Christ (John 6. 66; 2 Tim. 1. 15; Job 19. 13–19). Now a man is as forlorn as a pelican in the wilderness, as an owl in the desert, or as a sparrow upon the housetop. If a man cannot now go to the throne of grace by prayer, through Christ, and so fetch grace for his support from thence, what can he do? He cannot live of himself (John 15. 4). Wherefore this is a sore evil.

10. Another time of need is the day of death, when I am to pack up and to be gone from hence, the way of all the earth. Now the greatest trial is come, excepting that of the day of judgment. Now a man is to be stripped of all but that which

cannot be shaken. Now a man grows near the borders of eternity. Now he begins to see into the borders of the next world. Now death is death, and the grave the grave indeed! Now he begins to see what it is for body and soul to part, and what to go and appear before God (Eccles. 12. 5). Now the dark entry, and the thoughts of what is in the way from a deathbed to the gate of the holy heaven, comes nearer the heart than when health and prosperity do compass a man about. Wherefore this is like to be a trying time, a time of need indeed. A prudent man will make it one of the great concerns of his whole life, to get and lay up a stock of grace for this day, though the fool will rage and be confident: for he knows all will be little enough to keep him warm in his soul, while cold death strokes his hand over his face, and over his heart, and is turning his blood into jelly; while strong death is loosing his silver cord, and breaking his golden bowl (Eccles. 12. 6). Wherefore, I say, this motive wears a spur on its heel, a spur to prick us on to the throne of grace for mercy, and grace to help in time of need.

Continual supplies of grace are essential to our welfare

I come now to the next thing, which is, to show *that nothing can carry us through our needy times, but a continual supply of mercy and grace.* This the text fully implies, because it directs us to the throne of grace, for mercy and grace for that very end. And had there been any thing else that could have done it, the apostle would have made mention of it, and would also have directed the saints unto it. But forasmuch as he here makes mention of the needy time, and directs them to the throne of grace for mercy and grace to help, it follows that mercy and grace, and that only, can help us in the evil time.

Now mercy and grace are to be distinctly considered. 1. Mercy, for by it we have through Christ the continuation and multiplication of forgiveness, without which there is no salvation. 2. Grace, for by it we are upheld, supported, and enabled to go through our needy times, as Christians, without which there is no salvation either. The first all will grant, the second is clear: 'If any man draw back, my soul shall have no pleasure in him; but we are not of them who draw back unto perdition, but of them that believe to the saving of the soul' (Heb. 10. 38, 39).

1. Mercy is that by which we are pardoned, even all the falls, faults, failings, and weaknesses, that attend us, and that we are incident to, in this our day of temptation; and for this mercy we should pray, and say, 'Our Father, forgive us our trespasses' (Matt. 6. 9–12). For though mercy is free in the exercise of it to us-ward, yet God will have us ask, that we may have; as he also says in the text, 'Let us come boldly unto the throne of grace, that we may obtain mercy.' Here then we have one help, and that is, the mercy of God is to be extended to us from his throne through Jesus Christ, for our pardon and forgiveness in all those weaknesses that we are attended with in the needy or evil times; and we should come to God for this very thing. This is that which David means, when he says, 'Surely goodness and mercy shall follow me all the days of my life, and I will dwell in the house of the Lord for ever' (Ps. 23. 6). And again, 'When I said my foot slippeth; thy mercy, O Lord, held me up' (Ps. 94. 18). Set me clear and free from guilt, and from the imputation of sin unto death, by Christ.

Nor can any thing help where this is wanting; for our parts, our knowledge, our attainments, our graces, cannot so carry us through this world, but that we shall be guilty of that that will sink us down to hell, without God's pardoning mercy. It is not the grace that we have received can do it, nor the grace that is to be received that can do it; nothing can do it but the pardoning mercy of God; for because all our graces are here imperfect, they cannot produce a spotless obedience. But where there is not a spotless obedience, there must of necessity follow a continuation of pardon and forgiveness by mercy, or I know what will become of the soul. Here, therefore, the apostle lays an obligation upon you to come to the throne of grace, that you may obtain mercy, a continuation of mercy, mercy as long as you are like to live this vain life on the earth; mercy that will reach through all your days. For there is not a day, nor a duty; not a day that you live, nor a duty that you do, but will need that mercy should come after to take away your iniquity. Nay, you can not receive mercy so clearly, as not to stand in need of another act of mercy to pardon weakness in your no better receiving the last. We receive not our mercies so humbly, so readily, so gladly, and with that thankfulness as we should: and therefore, for the want of these, we have the need of another, and yet another act of God's sin-pardoning mercy, and need shall we have thereof, as long as evil time shall last with us.

But is not this great grace, that we should thus be called upon to come to God for mercy? Yea, is not God unspeakably good, in providing such a throne of grace, such a sacrifice, such a high priest, and so much mercy for us, and then to invite us to come with boldness to him for it? Nay, does not his kindness yet further appear, by giving of us items and intimations of needy times and evil days, on purpose to provoke us to come to him for mercy? This then shows us, as also we have hinted before, that the throne of grace, and Christ Jesus our high priest, are both provided upon the account of our imperfections, namely, that we who are called might not be, by remaining weaknesses, hindered of, but obtain eternal inheritance. Such weaknesses remain in the justified, and such slips and failings are found in and upon them, that call for a course of mercy and forgiveness to attend them. Further, this also intimates, that God's people should not be dejected at the apprehensions of their imperfections; I say, not so dejected, as therefore to cast off faith, and hope, and prayer; for a throne of grace is provided for them, to the which they may, they must, they ought continually to resort for mercy, sin-pardoning mercy.

2. As we are here to obtain mercy, so we are here to find grace. They that obtain mercy, shall find grace; therefore they are put together. That they may obtain mercy and find grace. Only they must find mercy first; for as forgiveness at first goes before sanctification in the general, so forgiveness afterwards goes before particular acts of grace for further sanctification. God gives not the spirit of grace to those that he has not first forgiven by mercy, for the sake of Christ. Also so long as he as a

Father forbears to forgive us as his adopted, so long we go without those further additions of grace that are here suggested in the text. But when we have obtained mercy to forgive, then we also find grace to our renewing. Therefore he says, First obtain mercy, and then find grace.

Grace here I take to be that grace which God has appointed for us, to dwell in us; and that by and through the continual supply of which we are to be enabled to do and suffer, and to manage ourselves in doing and suffering according to the will of God. 'Let us have grace whereby we may serve God acceptably with reverence and godly fear' (Heb. 12. 28). So again, 'he giveth more grace; wherefore he saith, God resisteth the proud, but giveth grace unto the humble' (James 4. 6; Prov. 3. 34; 1 Pet. 5. 5). The grace, therefore, that this text intends, is grace given or to be given; grace received or to be received; grace a root, a principle of grace, with its continual supplies for the perfecting of that salvation that God has designed for us. This was that which comforted Paul, when the messenger of Satan was sent to buffet him and it was said unto him by Christ, 'My grace is sufficient for thee' (2 Cor. 12. 9). As if Christ should say, Paul, be not utterly cast down, I have wherewith all to make you stand, and overcome, and that is my grace, by which you shall be supported, strengthened, comforted, and made to live a triumphant life, notwithstanding all that oppress you. But this came to him upon his praying; for this I prayed to God thrice, says he. So again, 'God is able to make all grace abound toward you; that ye always having all sufficiency in all things, may abound to every good work' (2 Cor. 9. 8). Thus you see, that by grace in these places is meant that spirit, and those principles of grace, by the increase and continual supply of which we are inwardly strengthened, and made to abound to every good work.

This then is the conclusion: That as there is mercy to be obtained by us at the throne of grace, for the pardon of all our weaknesses, so there is also grace there to be found that will yet strengthen us more, to all good walking and living before him. He gives more grace, and they that shall reign in life by one Jesus Christ receive one time or another abundance of grace. This then teaches us several things, some of which I will mention.

What this should teach us

1. That nature, as nature, is not capable of serving God: no, not nature where grace dwells, as considered abstract from that grace that dwells in it. Nothing can be done aright without grace; I mean, no part nor piece of gospel-duty. 'Let us have grace whereby we may serve God acceptably.' Nature, managed by grace, seasoned with grace, and held up with grace, can serve God acceptably. Let us have grace, seek for and find grace to do so; for we cannot do so but by grace: 'By the grace of God I am what I am; and his grace which was bestowed upon me, was not in vain; but I laboured more abundantly than they all; yet not I, but the grace of God which was with me' (1 Cor. 15. 10). What can be more plain than this beautiful text? For the apostle here quite shuts out nature, sanctified nature, for he indeed was a sanctified man, and concludes that even he, as of himself, did nothing of all the great works that he did; but they were done by the grace of God that was in him. Wherefore nature, sanctified nature, as nature, can of itself do nothing to the pleasing of God the Father.

Is not this the experience of all the godly? Can they do that at all times which they can do at some times? Can they pray, believe, love, fear, repent, and bow before God always alike? No. Why so? they are the same men, the same human nature, the same saints. Aye, but the same grace, in the same degree, operation, and life of grace, does not so now work on that man, that nature, that saint; therefore, notwithstanding he is what he is, he cannot do at all times alike. Thus therefore it is manifest that nature, simply as such, is a great way off from doing that which is acceptable with God. Refined, purified, sanctified nature, cannot do but by the immediate supplies, lifts, and helps of that spirit and principle of grace by the which it is so sanctified.

2. As nature, even where grace is, cannot, without the assist-

[161]

ance of that grace, do anything acceptable before God, so grace received, if it be not also supplied with more grace, cannot cause that we continue to do acceptable service to God. This also is clear by the text. For he speaks there to them that had received grace; yea, puts himself into the number, saying, 'Let us come boldly unto the throne of grace, that we may find grace to help in time of need.' If grace received would do, what need of more? What need we pray for more? What need we go to the throne of grace for more? This very exhortation says it will not: present supplies of grace are proportioned to our present need, and to help us to do a present work or duty. But is our present need all the need that we are like to have, and the present work all the work that we have to do in the world? Even so, the grace that we have received at present, though it can help us to do a present work, cannot, without a further supply, help us to do what is to be done hereafter. Wherefore, the apostle says, that his continuing to do was through his obtaining help, continual help of God: 'Having, therefore,' says he, 'obtained help of God, I continue unto this day, witnessing both to small and great' (Acts 26. 22). There must be a daily imploring of God for daily supplies from him, if we will do our daily business as we should.

A present dispensation of grace is like a good meal, a seasonable shower, or a penny in one's pocket, all which will serve for the present necessity. But will that good meal that I ate last week, enable me, without supply, to do a good day's work in this? or will that seasonable shower which fell last year, be, without further supplies, a seasonable help to the grain and grass that is growing now? or will that penny that supplied my want the other day, I say, will the same penny also, without a further supply, supply my wants to-day? The same may, I say, be said of grace received; it is like the oil in the lamp, it must be fed, it must be added to. And, there shall be a supply, for 'he giveth more grace' (James 4. 6). Grace is the sap, which from the root maintains the branches: stop the sap, and the branch will wither. Not that the sap shall be stopped where there is union, not stopped altogether; for as from the root the branch is supplied, so from Christ is every member furnished with a continual supply of grace, if it does as it should; 'of his fulness have all we received, and grace for grace' (John 1. 16).

The day of grace is the day of expense: this is our spending time. Hence we are called pilgrims and strangers in the earth, that is, travellers from place to place, from state to state, from trial to trial (Heb. 11. 13). Now, as the traveller at a fresh inn is made to spend fresh money, so Christians, at a fresh temptation, at a new temptation, are made to spend afresh, and a new supply of grace. Great men, when and while their sons are travellers, appoint that their bags of money be lodged ready, or conveniently paid in at such and such a place, for their suitable relief; and so they meet with supplies. Why, so are the sons of the Great One, and he has allotted that we should travel beyond sea, or at a great distance from our Father's house: wherefore he has appointed that grace shall be provided for us, to supply at such a place, such a state or temptation, as need requires. But withal, as my lord expects that his son should acquaint him with the present emptiness of his purse, and with the difficulty he has now to grapple with, so God our Father expects that we should plead by Christ our need at the throne of grace, in order to a supply of grace: 'Let us therefore come boldly unto the throne of grace, that we may obtain mercy, and find grace to help in time of need.'

Now then, this shows the reason why many Christians that are indeed possessed with the grace of God, do yet walk so oddly, act so poorly, and live such ordinary lives in the world. They are like those gentlemen's sons that are of the more extravagant sort, that walk in their lousy hue,[1] when they might be maintained better. Such young men care not, perhaps scorn to acquaint their fathers with their wants, and therefore walk in their threadbare jackets, with hose and shoes out at heels! A right emblem of the uncircumspect child of God! This also shows the reason of all those dreadful falls and miscarriages that many of the saints sustain; they made it not their business to watch to see what is coming, and to pray for a

[1] lousy hue = mean appearance.

supply of grace to uphold them. They, with David, are too careless, or, with Peter, too confident, or, with the disciples, too sleepy, and so the temptation comes upon them, and their want like an armed man. This also shows the reason why some that, to one's thinking, would fall every day—for that their want of parts, their small experience, their little knowledge of God's matters, do seem to bespeak it—yet stand, walk better, and keep their garments more white than those that have, when compared with them, twice as much as they. They are praying saints, they are often at the throne of grace, they are sensible of their weakness, keep a sight of their danger before their faces, and will not be contented without more grace.

3. And this leads me, in the third place, to show you, that were we wise, and did we ply it at the throne of grace for grace, as we should, O what spotless lives might we live! We should then always have help in time of need; for so the text insinuates, 'That we may obtain mercy, and find grace to help in time of need.' This is that which Peter means, when he says, 'And besides this,' that is, besides your faith in Christ, and besides your happy state of justification, 'giving all diligence, add to your faith, virtue; and to virtue, knowledge; and to knowledge, temperance; and to temperance, patience; and to patience, godliness; and to godliness, brotherly kindness; and to brotherly kindness, charity. For if these things be in you and abound,' and be continually supplied with a supply from the throne of grace, 'they make you that ye shall neither be barren nor unfruitful in the knowledge of our Lord Jesus Christ. But he that lacketh these things is blind, and cannot see afar off, and hath forgotten that he was purged from his old sins. Wherefore the rather, brethren, give diligence to make your calling and election sure: for if ye do these things, ye shall never fall: for so an entrance shall be ministered unto you abundantly into the everlasting kingdom of our Lord and Saviour Jesus Christ' (2 Pet. 1. 5–11).

The greatest part of professors now-a-days take up their time in contracting guilt, and asking for pardon, and yet are not much the better. Whereas, if they had but the grace to add to their faith, virtue, &c., they might have more peace, live better lives, and not have their heads so often in a bag as they have. 'To him that ordereth his conversation aright, will I show the salvation of God' (Ps. 50. 23). To him that disposeth his way aright. Now this cannot be done without a constant supplicating at the throne of grace for more grace. This then is the reason why every new temptation that comes upon you, so foils, so overcomes you, that you will need a new conversion, to be recovered from under the power and guilt that cleaves to you by its overshadowing of you. A new temptation, a sudden temptation, an unexpected temptation, usually foils those that are not upon their watch; and that have not been before with God to be inlaid with grace proportionable to what may come upon them.

'That ye may find grace to help in time of need!' There is grace to be found at the throne of grace that will help us under the greatest straits. 'Seek and ye shall find'; it is there, and it is to be found there; it is to be found there of the seeking soul, of the soul that seeketh him. Wherefore I will conclude as I did begin: 'Let us therefore come boldly unto the throne of grace that we may obtain mercy, and find grace to help in time of need.'

6

CONCLUSION

━━━

We will now speak something by way of conclusion, and so wind up the whole.

Six lessons to be learned from this text

1. You must remember that we have been hitherto speaking of the throne of grace, and showing what it is; that we have also been speaking of Christ's sacrifice, and how he manages his high priest's office before the throne of grace. We have also here been speaking of the mercy and grace that is to be obtained and found at this throne of grace, and of what advantage it is to us in this our pilgrimage. Now, from all this it follows that sin is a fearful thing: for all this ado is, that men might be saved from sin! What a devil then is sin: it is the worst of devils; it is worse than all devils; those that are devils, sin hath made them so; nor could anything else have made them devils but sin.

Now, I pray, what is it to be a devil, but to be under, for ever, the power and dominion of sin, an implacable spirit against God? From this implacableness all the power in heaven and earth cannot release them, because God of his justice has bound them over to judgment. These spirits are by sin carried quite away from themselves, as well as from God that made them; they cannot design their own good; they cannot leave that which yet they know will be everlastingly mischievous to themselves. Sin has bound them to itself so fast, that there can be no deliverance for them, but by the Son of God, who also has refused them, and left them to themselves, and to the judgment which they have deserved. Sin also has got a victory over man, has made him an enemy to God and to his own salvation; has caught him, captivated him, carried away his mind, and will, and heart, from God, and made him choose to be vain, and to run the hazard of eternal damnation, with rejoicing and delight. But God left not men where he left those wicked spirits, namely, under the everlasting chains of darkness, reserved unto judgment; but devised means for their ransom and reconciliation to himself; which is the thing that has been discoursed of in the foregoing part of this book. But, I say, what a thing is sin, what a devil and master of devils is it, that it should, where it takes hold, so hang that nothing can unclinch its hold but the mercy of God and the heart-blood of his dear Son!

O the fretting, eating, infecting, defiling, and poisonous nature of sin, that it should so eat into our flesh and spirit, body and soul, and so stain us with its vile and stinking nature. Yea, it has almost turned man into the nature of itself; insomuch as that sometimes, when nature is mentioned, sin is meant; and when sin is mentioned, nature is meant (Eph. 2. 3; 5. 8). Wherefore sin is a fearful thing, a thing to be lamented, a thing to be abhorred, a thing to be fled from with more astonishment and trembling than one would fly from any devil, because it is the worst of things. It is that without which nothing can be bad, and because where it takes hold it so fastens that nothing, as I have said, can release whom it has made a captive, but the mercy of God and the heart-blood of his dear Son. O what a thing is sin!

2. As by what has been said, sin appears to be exceeding sinful, so, from hence it also follows, that the soul is a precious thing. For you must know that all this is for the redemption of the soul. The redemption of the soul is precious (Ps. 49. 8, 20). I say, it is for the redemption of the soul; it was for this that Christ was made a priest, a sacrifice, an altar, a throne of grace, yea, sin, a curse, and what not, that was necessary for our deliverance from sin, and death, and everlasting damnation. He that would know what a soul is, let him read in letters of

blood the price and purchase of the soul. It was not for a light, a little, an inconsiderable thing, that Christ Jesus underwent what he suffered when he was in the world, and gave himself a ransom for souls. No, no! The soul is a great, a vast great thing, notwithstanding it is so little set by of some. Some prefer anything that they fancy, above the soul; a slut,[1] a lie, a pot, an act of fraudulency, the swing of a prevailing passion, anything shall be preferred when the occasion offers itself. If Christ had set as little by souls as some men do, he had never left his Father's bosom, and the glory that he had with him; he had never so humbled himself, so gave himself to punishment, affliction, and sorrow; and made himself so the object of scorn, and contempt, and reproach, as he did, and all that the souls of sinners might live a life in glory with him.

But methinks this is the mystery of all as to this, that the soul should take such pains, contrive such ways, and take such advantages against itself! For it is the soul that sins, that the soul might die! O! sin, what art thou? What hast thou done? and what still wilt thou further do, if mercy, and blood and grace, doth not prevent thee? O silly soul! what a fool has sin made of thee? what an ass art thou become to sin? that ever an immortal soul, at first made in the image of God, for God, and for his delight, should so degenerate from its first station, and so abase itself that it might serve sin, as to become the devil's ape, and to play like a Jack Pudding[2] for him upon any stage or theatre in the world! But I recall myself; for if sin can make one who was sometimes a glorious angel in heaven, now so to abuse himself as to become, to appearance, as a filthy frog, a toad, a rat, a cat, a fly, a mouse, a dog, or bitch's whelp,[3] to serve its ends upon poor mortals, that it might gull them of everlasting life, no marvel if the soul is so beguiled as to sell itself from God, and all good, for so poor a nothing as a momentary pleasure is.

[1] slut = a woman of loose character.
[2] Jack Pudding = a buffoon or mountebank.
[3] It was in Bunyan's time the universally received opinion that Satan appeared in the shape of animals to allure poor wretches into sin.

3. If sin and the soul are such great things, then behold the love and care of God; his love to souls, the care he has taken to deliver them from sin. Sin, as I have said, is such a thing as from which no man can deliver himself; the soul is such a thing, so rich and valuable in its nature, that scarce one in twenty thousand counts of it as they should. But God, the lover of mankind, and the greatest enemy to sin, has provided means effectually to overthrow the one, and to save and secure the other. Behòld, therefore, the love of God, the care of God for us; for when we neither loved nor cared for ourselves, God both loved us and cared for us. God commended his love towards us in sending his Son to be the propitiation for our sins.

Let it be then concluded that 'God is love,' and that the love that God hath to us is such as we never had for ourselves. We have been often tried about our own love to ourselves, and it has been proved over, and over, and over, that sometimes even we that are Christians could, and would, had it been possible, have pawned ourselves, our souls, and our interest in Christ, for a foul and beastly lust. But God, who is rich in mercy, for his great love wherewith he loved us, would not suffer it so to be. Now, if we are so fickle and uncertain in our love to ourselves, as to value our salvation at so low and so base a rate, can it be imagined that ever we should, had it been left to our choice, have given the best of what we have for the salvation of our souls? Yet God gave his Son to be the Saviour of the world. I say again, if our love is so slender to our own souls, can any think that it should be more full to the souls of others? And yet God had such love to us, as to give his only begotten Son for our sins. Yet again, how should it be that we, who are usually so affected with the conceit of our own happiness, since we care no more for our own souls, do our best to secure the souls of others? and yet God, who is infinitely above all creatures, has so condescended, as to concern himself, and to give the best of his flock, even his only beloved Son, for very dust and ashes. Wherefore, 'Herein is love, not that we loved God,' or our neighbour, 'but that God loved us, and sent his Son to be the propitiation for our sins' (1 John 4. 10).

4. Is sin so vile a thing? is the soul so precious a thing? and is God's love and care of the salvation of the souls of sinners infinitely greater than is their own care for their own souls? Then this should teach those concerned to blush, to blush, I say, and to cover their faces with shame. There is nothing, as I know of, that more becomes a sinner, than blushing and shame does; for he is the harbourer, the nurse, and the nourisher of that vile thing called sin, that so great an enemy of God, and that so great an enemy to the soul. It becomes him also, if he considers what a creature God has made him, and how little he has set by his own creation, and by the matter of which God has made his soul. Let him also consider unto what base things he has stooped and prostrated himself, while things infinitely better have stood by and offered themselves unto him freely; yea, how he has cast that God that made him, and his Son that came to redeem him, quite behind his back, and before their faces embraced, loved, and devoted himself unto him that seeks nothing more than the damnation of his soul.

Ah, Lord! when will foolish man be wise, and come to God with his hands upon his head, and with his face covered with shame, to ask him forgiveness for that wickedness which he has committed! which is wickedness committed not only against holiness and justice, against which also men by nature have an antipathy, but against mercy and love, without which man cannot tell what to do. Blush, sinner, blush. O that you had grace to blush! But this is God's complaint, 'Were they ashamed when they had committed abomination? Nay, they were not at all ashamed, neither could they blush' (Jer. 8. 12). It is a sad thing that men should be thus void of consideration, and yet they are so. They are at a continual jest with God and his Word, with the devil and sin, with hell and judgment. But they will be in earnest one day; but that one day will be too late!

5. Is it so that God, though sin is so fearful a thing, has prepared an effectual remedy against it, and purposed to save

us from the evil and damning effects thereof? Then this should beget thankfulness in the hearts of the godly, for they are made partakers of this grace; I say, it should beget thankfulness in their hearts. 'Thanks be unto God for his unspeakable gift,' said the apostle, when he seriously thought of that which was much inferior to what we have been discoursing of (2 Cor. 9. 15). That was about men's willingness to do good; this is about God's. That was about men's willingness to give money to poor saints; this about God's willingness to give Christ Jesus his Son to the world. It was the thoughts of this redemption and salvation that made David say, 'Bless the Lord, O my soul, and all that is within me, bless his holy name' (Ps. 103. 1). O! they that are partakers of redeeming grace, and that have a throne of grace, a covenant of grace, and a Christ, that is the Son of God's love, to come to, and to live by, should be a thankful people! 'By him therefore let us offer the sacrifice of praise to God continually, giving thanks in his name' (Heb. 13. 15). How many obligations has God laid upon his people, to give thanks to him at every remembrance of his holiness!

Study the priesthood, the high priesthood of Jesus Christ, both the first and second part thereof. The first part was that when he offered up himself without the gate, when he bare our sins in his own body on the tree. The second part is that which he executes there whither he is now gone, even in heaven itself, where the throne of grace is. I say, study what Christ has done, and is a-doing. O! what is he a-doing now? With his priestly robes on, he is sprinkling his blood before the throne of grace; that is too little thought on by the saints of God: 'We have such a high priest, who is set on the right hand of the throne of the Majesty in the heavens, a minister of the sanctuary, and of the true tabernacle, which the Lord pitched, and not man' (Heb. 8. 1, 2). Busy thyself, fellow-Christian, about this blessed office of Christ. It is full of good, it is full of sweet, it is full of heaven, it is full of relief and succour for the tempted and dejected; wherefore, I say again, study these things, give thyself wholly to them.